I0123387

The Key to Life

How to get more out of chastity for men

Christopher Charlton

EmOhErotica
Leeds UK

The Key to Life
How to get more out of chastity for men

Chris Charlton
Published by EmOh Erotica, Yorkshire, Europe – 2015
ISBN: 978-1-873031-47-6

Published by EmOh Erotica, PO Box HP346, Leeds LS6 1UL, UK

British Library Cataloguing-in-Publication data: Christopher Charlton
The Key to Life; How to get more of chastity for men,
1. Title
ISBN   978-1-873031-47-6 (paperback)
            978-1-873031-45-2 (Kindle update 2015)

Cover design: Ben Matthews

TO

… the man who becomes my
husband because he appreciates that
a chastity device is the ultimate
wedding band

CHRISTOPHER CHARLTON

CONTENTS

THE KEY TO LIFE

ACKNOWLEDGEMENTS

I would like to thank several guys who have contributed to my appreciation of chastity (and 'power play') over the years and my sexual education. They include Master H for keyholding (at times) and other supervision, Locked 57 for all his research and running the Lockedmen website, the late Pandy (S) for introducing me to belt designs, 'Wolf', Wes, Mike P for his patience and assisting with the presentation from which this book emerged, Gordon H (for buying me my first cage), to Dieter at Steelworxx and Walter Goethals for making me great devices and Chris at Steelwerks Extreme for his great imagination and inspiration.

Christopher Charlton
2015

Introduction
WHAT AM I GETTING INTO?

When I first took a chastity device to an SM run for gay men in the United States some time in the 1990s to try to boost sales for the friend who was making them, I described the effect as 'changing a scene into a way of life'.

In the pre-internet days, finding out about such devices – like so much of the more diverse and esoteric aspects of human sexuality – was difficult. You had to get to know someone who knew someone who may, once they trusted you enough, introduce you to a third or fourth person who could actually put you in touch with one of the few people who were making such devices then. (Lyricist Herbert Farjeon, who wrote the song *I've danced with a man, who's danced with a girl, who's danced with the Prince of Wales,* had probably had a similar experience.)

Chastity was the same. If you were lucky, you found someone who – eventually – would reveal that they had a similar interest and you could talk, and hopefully learn, more. Finding someone in the 1980s who actually had a device of some sort or another was additional difficulty.

Since then, the more I have experienced and the more I have thought about 'chastity', the more complex the topic has become. That personal perception should not, however, deter anyone from starting to think about chastity, what it means for them and how they can explore the beautiful paradox of the physical and psychological excitement that can result from being locked or locking another (guy).

That said, many probably thoroughly enjoy chastity without thinking about it too deeply. For others, understanding the psychology – from various perspectives – enhances the experience, because they can relish what is happening to them personally while vicariously trying to imagine what is going on in the mind (or between the legs) of another person.

As a gay man, my experience with chastity – both while being locked and having locked others – had been solely in that (homosexual) context. However, while researching the topic more thoroughly, the realization dawned that the gender of the person doing the locking (hereinafter, as the lawyers write, known metaphorically as the *keyholder*) is frequently irrelevant. The psychological effects are very, very similar regardless of whether the keyholder is male or female. The practicalities facing a gay man when he is presented with a device are the same as those of his heterosexual counterpart.

Indeed, these thoughts were first pulled together for an event for gay men – and remain significantly based on such experiences and evidence. Indeed, the sub-title very nearly included the word 'gay' before 'men', but a friend – rightly – pointed out that sexual orientation is a secondary aspect to the emotions and behaviors being documented and explored here. Why? Some men who identify as heterosexual hold keys for others who see themselves as gay while some heterosexual men who seek locking have gay male keyholders. Consequently, the focus therefore reflects perspectives relevant to gay and straight 'lockees' and gay 'lockers' but omits some aspects of locking by females.

This volume is an attempt to pull together personal thoughts and experiences with those of others – recounted individually and online as a single source of useful information for those who are starting out while also, I hope, offerings some practical and psychological suggestions for the more experienced. This comes from the perspective of vain optimism that they may either avoid the disappointment that can emerge if relationships reach the status of being taken for granted or find renewed excitement and vigor by varying or adding required behaviors and activities to the interaction. Also, as more friends – and those who inhabit online chat rooms and various chastity websites – realized that I was regarded by some kink peers in the US as having some knowledge of the subject, and by implication, some authority it seems, I have been receiving more and more fairly basic questions.

Indeed, just as I was trying to finish this book, I opened my e-mails one morning to discover a message from a very close kink buddy saying: 'My friend ... wants to get a chastity device that doesn't require any piercings, but will be effective enough for two weeks prior to a play session. Do you have any suggestions?'

My initial reaction was to say 'wait for this book to appear'. My second is, now that it is available and you have started to read it, that the question is far more complex than those asking it ever appreciate. So many factors need to be identified – and then taken into consideration – when thinking about a device that I feel justified in having tried to pull as many of these together as I can. My academic experience is, compared to some, limited – but I remember vividly my introduction to methodology: 'identify the variables, and then eliminate them'. Said in the wrong voice, this could sound as if I am advocating that the Daleks destroy every university in the world, but the approach is extremely valid here. Many people seem to have difficulties dealing with abstract concepts; identifying the variables and then eliminating them is perhaps most valid when the approach is *applied* to chastity.

Indeed, taking chastity seriously – and making locking part of your life (or someone else's) can be expensive. Lots of designs have become available since the 1990s, but the most sophisticated, custom-made devices can be very expensive, although simultaneously represent excellent value for that money.

Huge quantities of information are available online – but most is very personal and subjective. While some empirical research has been carried out, it is relatively limited and has not gone through rigorous academic scrutiny. Therefore, this book is an attempt to pull some of those observations together and find some consensus in otherwise random and scattered beliefs and experiences.

So, if you're thinking about trying a device, being locked or locking someone else, then please read on; you have a lot to think about.

Part I
THE THINKING

Terminology and the social climate

'Chastity' as a word is bandied around, often without sufficient consideration of what is actually meant (by those using the term) or understood (by those hearing or reading it). So, for the sake of clarity from the start, defining the concept seems essential.

For some, chastity means no more than depriving a person of the ability to penetrate or be penetrated sexually rather than eliminating all sexual release or, alternatively, the ability to touch the cock.

The human – male – condition varies greatly too. Some guys can achieve orgasm even while locked in quite 'heavy' devices, such as those like the Carrara which may cover the male genitals completely. Such men may not ejaculate, but they can experience the sensations of an orgasm through, for example, anal stimulation, either as a learned or trained response – ranging from being fucked to the stimulation of the prostate gland, during fucking or by using one or more fingers, 'insertables' such as dildos or electric butt plugs or more gentle massaging of the internal membranes.

Ejaculation is regarded here as 'shooting', ejecting seminal fluid under pressure from the penis. For most men, ejaculation and orgasm appear synonymous and simultaneous. For those exploring chastity, the difference can become apparent relatively quickly.

Some men can ejaculate without their penises being touched or stimulated directly in any way whatsoever, either erect or not. Others may achieve orgasm, become erect and ejaculate as an effect of playing with their balls, perhaps with electrical stimulation or simply by tugging on the scrotum in a way that mimics masturbation. Some may achieve a 'ball-gasm' while the penis is flaccid. They may not ejaculate at all while others do 'discharge' some semen, but as little more than a dribble, even though their bodies may experience the muscular tension then rapid relaxation that, for most, defines an orgasm. Some men can even, for example, achieve orgasm when their nipples are aroused and stimulated, without any genital contact whatsoever.

So, for one person, the only limit set by 'chastity', with a device such as a very large and impractical penis piercing, may be to prevent active penetration while allowing masturbation. For another, the challenge may be to redirect the psychological conditioning of adolescence towards orgasm as represented by ejaculation to achieving a similar effect from anal stimulation, with the cock remaining flaccid within a device.

Some men lock themselves – for a variety of reasons. These could range from trying to prevent themselves masturbating or maintaining a level of horniness, just in case the opportunity for sex appears.

However, in many circumstances (at least for discussion here), accepting that chastity is an activity – or denial thereof – usually involving two people, the limitations should – as far as possible – be identified at the outset and realistic expectations established between those involved. While primarily focusing on chastity for men through the control of the penis (and the ability to penetrate others sexually), chastity may also – as another section of this book will consider – encompass control of the ability to be penetrated.

For some, chastity means no more than depriving a person of the ability to penetrate or be penetrated sexually rather than eliminating all sexual release or, alternatively, the ability to touch the penis.

In such circumstances, accepting that chastity is an activity – or restriction thereof – involving two people, the limitations should – as far as possible – be identified at the outset and realistic expectations established. (Additionally, for many enthusiasts, chastity is not about total *denial* per se, but about the *restriction* of access to physical sexual stimulation, certainly of the penis, but for some, also the entire male genitals and anal penetration.)

For some, chastity is short-term – with periods of locking ranging from a relatively short few hours to a few weeks. Others desire to be locked permanently – for any number or combination of the reasons for wanting chastity that will become apparent in this book.

The very words associated with chastity are – like so much around kink – laden with connotations that reflect social uptightness.

The English words, again like so many, have evolved from Latin. In this case, the words are castum – meaning 'pure' – and agare, meaning to 'compel to be'. That, in the 21st century, seems a more accurate reflection of chastity in this context than some of the terms that have appeared, according to Collins dictionary, since the 17th century. Collins says that to *chastise* means to punish, especially by beating, or to scold severely. To chasten, the dictionary suggests, is to (a) bring to a 'state of submission', to subdue or tame; (b) to discipline or correct by punishment or (c) to moderate, to restrain or to temper.

For those who like to lock (or put someone else in chastity) or be locked (in chastity), the concept of 'purity' – reflecting submission and compulsion – is, as will become increasingly apparent, probably more appropriate than much to do with *punishment*. (Nevertheless, those who constrain others, usually with devices that have locks so they are called *keyholders*, may decide to extend locking times as either stick-or-carrot incentives for those they have locked.)

Although humanity has collected – and disseminated – far more information about sexual behavior in the last decades of the 20th century and the first of the 21st, empirical evidence about aspects of chastity is still very limited. What is presented here is the dilution of anecdotal reports, collected informally over many years. That the connotations of the Latin words from which current terminology has derived seem more in tune with the understanding of the 2010s may be seen as ironic – and, perhaps over optimistically, a rejection of the ignorance, prejudice and political censure of 19th century establishment figures, both in Europe and the United States.

Perhaps too this look to the past can mean that terminology is less of an obstacle to understanding the complications and apparent paradoxes and incongruities around sexual arousal and conditioning than we may initially imagine. Nevertheless, those who consider sex to be recreational rather than entirely procreational may find many of these concepts alien. Alex Comfort in his pioneering book *The Joy of Sex* acknowledged that for many 'sex' per se was vaginal penetration and that anything else was 'merely' foreplay. (Acknowledging this cultural convention can be politically challenging – as one consequence is that US President Bill Clinton was not lying when he said he 'did not have sex' with Monica Lewinsky; he was being culturally accurate and honest, despite what some would have us believe.)

Similarly, the expression 'slap and tickle' may have entered common usage in the United Kingdom decades ago but anything other than the missionary position for vaginal penetration can be difficult for some to perceive. The Marquis de Sade and Count von Sacher-Masoch have left a literary legacy that reflects the development of psychology when they were alive – well before the 21st century. (The Marquis lived from 1740 until 1814 and the Count from 1836 until 1895.)

Despite more recent perceptions, the 'Victorians' of the late 19th century could be as curious as they were reputedly prurient. Simultaneously, while some sought to use sexual repression for political purposes – a tactic that can be regarded as ferociously self-defeating when sexually transmitted infections later came close to undermining the British war effort between 1914 and 1918 – others were busily researching this aspect of human sexuality. Their efforts had to be shrouded in the social respectability of academic curiosity, but their work has provided a late 19th and early 20th century foundation on which others could build decades later.

In early 2015, for example, the UK Institute of Sexology staged a public exhibition at the Wellcome Institute in central London that revealed some of the investigations that had been done in the name of anthropology – often in 'the colonies' away from potential political discomfort. In Europe, the Austro-German psychiatrist (Richard Freiherr von) Krafft-Ebing is regarded as almost a father of this area of this area of study.

Figures such as Magnus Hirschfeld opened up a more humanitarian approach to homosexuality in late 19th century Germany – advocating that a greater scientific understanding of human sexuality could help eliminate hostility towards gays and others. In the UK, Havelock Ellis extended initial studies of homosexuality to include other sexual practices and 'inclinations'.

Notes produced for the 2015 exhibition in London said that 'gathering ... data from observation is central to the sexologist's craft. Expounders of this approach include Richard von Krafft-Ebing, who painstakingly documented cases of sexual "deviance", and Havelock Ellis, who attacked the hypocrisy of modern morals by citing candid accounts from history and literature and asking his friends to write their own sexual autobiographies.'

For those whose 'inclinations' may still be regarded by some as 'deviant', then the work of such realistic and liberal individuals should never be forgotten – as they were able to get themselves into such positions and carry out their work so diligently (within the methodological standards of the time) that they were very difficult for the advocates of repression to undermine.

Having the confidence to confront repression is never easy. A single individual may represent an easy target for censure and ridicule, but censuring groups is more difficult and less coherent. The world did not end when women were allowed to vote or when, in some jurisdictions, homosexual activity was decriminalized. One person's perversity is another's diversity. The imaginative expression of sexuality should be encouraged – as a route to overcoming psychological insecurity – and celebrated. That the psychologically immature remain vulnerable to repression and being stigmatized (especially in the name of organized religion) is a perpetual cultural and political challenge.

Therefore, while the word 'chastise' may still laden with negative connotations, these can change. Indeed, the term can yet be regarded as perpetuating the association of sexual denial with punishment or, alternatively, with enforced control, the absence of consent and a means to deter behaviors that a dominant figure does not want. If anything is clear from this book, then for the majority of people 'into' chastity in the 21st century in the west, chastity is exactly the opposite of this; it is about positivity, about consent and about expressing love. Reclaiming other terms has been a slow process that has taken years; perhaps the time has come for the words 'chastity' and 'chaste' to be reclaimed too.

Similarly, in an era of equality and human rights, being overt about the power dynamic within a relationship can be socially challenging. This is probably because aspects of the psychology and the expression of such needs are not yet widely appreciated or understood.

Most crucially, in the concept of chastity, the most important facet of this is consent. Those who are locked do so willingly. And, as can probably never be repeated too often, consent has its five dimensions – who, what, when, where and how. (The sixth – 'why' – will be explored more in the next part of this book dealing with the psychology of chastity.) The guy being locked assents to *who* – by agreeing who is in control of the key (even though that person might not always have it in their personal possession), *what* sort of device they are locked into, *when* and for how long they are locked, *where* locking does (or does not) take place and whether any rituals surround the locking itself and *how* this is achieved. Consent regarding time may only be given once – but it can last for hours, days, weeks, months, years or perhaps even forever. Similarly, the *where* dimension may include unlocking to go through airport security scanners.

The intensity of chastity that a person may experience could be quite great but – in this context – the key (for want of a word) lies in consent and the fact that the guy being locked has (although he may later regret the decision) agreed to it.

The history

Until the advent of the internet, the market for chastity devices was small and limited. In the United Kingdom, Hal Higginbotham was trading as Tollyboy, custom-making stainless steel belts from a small home workshop in Yorkshire. Although he was heterosexual, many of his clients were gay men, even then. The devices were expensive and produced as a hobby. Customers frequently had to wait a year or sometimes even longer for their orders to be fulfilled. When he died, his widow did transfer the design rights – but the brand does not seem to have flourished.

Hal's design for men had a downwards-pointing metal sheath for the penis and the balls were pushed out to the sides but most characteristic was his choice of rotary locks, produced in the United States.

In the US, another couple had created a virtual monopoly – trading as Access Denied and producing a design that was not too different from that coming slowly off Hal Higginbotham's lathes at the other side of the Atlantic.

Exchanging correspondence with Hal towards the end of his life and communicating with one of his clients, before then talking to Richard, an Australian who gained the rights to the designs and brand after Hal's death, it appeared that the morality of the use of some of the early devices would, to those committed to human rights and with a generally liberal outlook, be questionable to say the least. Some men appeared to have bought devices for wives and other women genuinely to prevent (vaginal) penetration in their absence. Men who bought them for themselves or for other men, and indeed, some women who were involved in the purchases too, seemed to consider erotic denial to be their greater priority.

One anonymous online writer has observed that – certainly for the 'early years' of the 1980s and 90s, steel devices were more likely to be made in Europe, until the CB (the brand of a) series of polycarbonate devices from the US became more widely available (and affordable). The explosion came when materials science and cheaper manufacturing costs coincided with the marketing potential of the internet. 'I doubt,' this man wrote, 'that entrepreneurs would invest in all that tooling (no pun intended) if the market wasn't expanding in leaps and bounds'.

As I have said, my first personal contact with a full chastity belt was with a friend who had a Tollyboy in the 1980s. Interest was at that time limited (like so much) in the years before the internet made contact so much easier. (While the UK may have taken a lead over some sorts of censorship with a landmark trial over publication of *Lady Chatterley's Lover* by DH Lawrence, access to anything esoteric was restricted by legislation covering 'obscene publications'. The establishment considered pornography, of any sort, to be a social evil until well into the 1970s. Importing US publications such as *Drummer* – which did so much to provide education as well as erotic reading regarding 'leathersex' and 'kink' – was illegal in the UK.

Getting an illicit copy of Larry Townsend's groundbreaking 1972 book *The Leatherman's Handbook* into the country was regarded as a major subversive achievement – and treasured copies were valued and carefully loaned around only the most trustworthy and genuinely interested of friends.)

The concept of chastity is mentioned incidentally in *The Leatherman's Handbook*. In talking about piercing, in the late 1960s and early 70s when Larry Townsend was working on the manuscript, this was truly an aspect of 'esoteric exotica'. In that chapter, he wrote: 'In some S&M combinations, a small padlock or metal ring may be fastened through a permanent hole in the foreskin or nipple. On the cock, it becomes a type of chastity belt; in either position, it causes the M (the masochist or submissive) to be constantly aware of its presence and the continued power of the person who placed it there.' He continued: 'The sensation of wearing the master's talisman is both a symbol of the M's submission and a reminder of his humiliated state. Just as an M may wear a chain about his neck, either locked in place or spot-welded, so he may enjoy bearing this brand of servitude.'

(Townsend's terminology may, after 40 further years or wider discussions of kink and power relationships, seem a little antiquated. The notions of 'humiliation' and 'servitude' have become dissociated from those of submission, per se, with the recognition that someone deferential may take pride in the dynamic between them and someone they regard as more dominant or assertive, just as these have in themselves been recognized as not being the same as liking to give or receive 'pain'.)

However, infibulation with a piercing of some sort through a foreskin, may make penetration slightly impractical – and potentially painful for the recipient (although that may, in itself, be an additional turn-on for some) – but not impossible. Masturbating without some 'additional' flesh along the shaft of the penis may be uncomfortable, to the extent of being a deterrent but, again, could be achieved. Locking together two permanent piercings may be more effective. Some men have padlocks through Prince Albert piercings that are locked to either guiches or scrotal piercings. (These piercings go through the urethral opening – or piss slit – in the glans and emerge through a small hole set below the penis head where it 'flares'.) Another, more radical, modification – featured in a photograph that circulated widely online – showed a larger ring, about an inch and a half (or 5 or 6 centimeters) in diameter and in a gauge of about 5/16ths of an inch (or 8millimetres) that ran through the penis to emerge through an opening in the urethra (called a *urethral reroute*) behind the scrotum. Penetration of another would have been impossible in any way and while the penis could have become engorged the 'erection' would have been directed downwards and around the ring.

Townsend discussed aspects of 'the castration complex', both real and symbolic, in *The Leatherman's Handbook II*, also first published in 1972. 'If,' he wrote, 'you were to make a survey of the unconscious fears shared by the entire population of human males, you would find the fear of castration among the highest, both in strength and frequency. Because the male genitals hang outside the body, they are most vulnerable to attack and damage (the overt fear) and to actual loss (covert, or subconscious, fear). Most of us are sophisticated enough to know, regardless of our Freudian anxieties, that the chance of actually losing our balls is fairly remote, so manifest no open concern. The majority of SM guys tend to sublimate this primordial anxiety into other, symbolic areas.'

While primarily considering this in terms of the balls as manifestations of masculinity, both physical and cultural, the same perspective can also be applied to the penis. Townsend added, of the balls: 'As so many other psychological phobias are turned inside-out in our games, so it is with the castration anxiety'. While Townsend was probably one of the very first to document these beautiful paradoxes of kink, the internet has allowed these to be explored and enjoyed by far more people. What has happened in the 40-some years between Townsend's writings and this 2014/15 analysis is that both the understanding of much of the psychology has been explored, by practitioners if not academics, and the technology available for making devices that are practical has advanced exponentially.

Hal Higginbotham, for example, got most (if not all) his work through word of mouth. He produced Tollyboy devices as a hobby, rather than as a business, so many months did often pass between placing an order and the custom-made device being ready. Technology – or its development at that time – contributed to the production time and cost. The stainless steel was expensive, especially when bought in small quantities. Waistbands and other components had to be cut, one at a time, using costly metalworking equipment, available only to amateurs with deep pockets or by gaining access to engineering business premises at weekends or outside normal business hours. For some, the rigidity of those designs, heavier steel that was more difficult to mould to the shape of the body, and pre-determined sizes that made no allowance for changes to anyone's waist size were also deterrents.

Chastity, per se, is now, noticeably absent from other key early contributions to the collective wisdom of kink. *Leathersex; A Guide for the Curious Outsider and the Serious Player*, written by one-time *Drummer* editor Joseph Bean, and published in 1994, has no mention of chastity in the index. Shortly after that, *Consensual Sadomasochism; How to talk about it and how to do it safely*, by William A Henkin PhD and Sybil Holiday CCSSE, similarly overlooked the topic. The comprehensive *On the Safe Edge, A Manual for SM Play*, by Trevor Jacques, and published in Toronto, Canada, in August 1993, does include two index entries – but for 'chastity belt'. One deals briefly with the device primarily as a means of keeping a butt plug in place – while the second mention, four paragraphs and a few hundred words, but nevertheless this does, looking back, seem a significant, early cultural recognition of chastity.

'Most people envision', wrote Trevor Jacques, 'a clanking, rusting device of vaguely medieval construction when they think of chastity belts. Most of the ones you can see in museums are of dubious origin, efficiency, and practicality. Today, they are used in SM play as a form of real or symbolic enforced fidelity. To surrender such personal freedoms can be very erotic. Wearing the belt at home during play is one thing, but how about going to work wearing a chastity belt? This could engender feelings of anticipation of the belt being discovered as well as the sense of dependence, ie hours of erotic excitement.

'If the aim is to prevent arousal or masturbation, you will be hard pressed to find one that works well,' he added, and but remembering that this was written in the early 1990s is important in terms of the context today. 'The problems relate to the variability of the situation, particularly in the male. A comfortable fit can rapidly become a dangerous one. Since many chastity belts are made of metal, their harshness and unforgiving nature may make everyday wearing impossible. As a fantasy or as part of a short scene, they may be fine, but for longer use you should consider the potential problems very carefully before you proceed. The fantasy of being welded into a cast iron jock strap is one thing; the reality of not being able to sit down in it without getting a hernia is another.

'One aspect of the appeal of chastity belts is visual. The belt may be made of metal and look medieval; or perhaps it could take on the look of a Victorian corset, all horsehide and rivets. What about those shining high-security ones in your local sex store? Another aspect is the degree of security: do you want to completely prevent masturbation, simply make sex difficult, or establish who belongs to whom? Yet another aspect is that of how long the device is to be worn. Some designs, although marketed with the suggestion that they could be practical for long periods, may be less secure than potential users would want.

'The psychological effects of wearing a device at home are different from those of being forced to wear it under clothing in a public place. The latter feelings are also very different from being forced to wear the belt in public without the cover of clothes. (As can easily be seen), the possibilities of the variety of chastity belts are almost limitless. They are determined only by your imagination and consideration of safety.'

A posting on a Fetlife forum in July or August 2014 asked about the relative popularity of chastity as 'a particular kink within the BDSM communities'. Is it, the questioner asked, 'becoming more popular or just more visible?' After wondering whether chastity was affected by trends and geographic or cultural variances, s/he also asked: 'Has it become more popular with the advance of mass-produced devices?'

The first response began with another question: 'Who knows?' before proceeding to make a key sociological point in a humorous way: 'Gallup hasn't released their latest survey data, so your guess is as good as mine.' That person's view was, however, that 'as kink awareness slowly grows, so does acceptance and the number of people participating.' So far, no evidence seems to have appeared which contradicts this basic hypothesis.

The contributions continued, with one person saying: 'I can only go back to the late 90s when I first started setting long-term wear chastity devices for sale. Full chastity belts are still pretty expensive, the design has gotten better over the years, but still require fittings and measurements, and were not designed to be modifiable or taken from one person and put onto another because of custom fitting. Some people don't like the idea of forking out several hundred dollars, wait for months for the product, and then run the risk of putting it on display rather than putting it on the sub because a sub gained or lost weight. The steel ones were almost entirely made in Europe until the lighter and less bulky CB series came along.'

Another added: 'Chastity is a different kind of kink that not everybody is into. I am noticing that the CB is becoming more visible in the community and increasingly more popular since these cage designs came out. I think that with the presence of 3D printing, that there will be other designers that will open up shop to offer more variety, better, or different designs and etc for cheaper.'

The psychological aspect came to the fore too, with another person saying: '(It) seems like it's becoming at least more visible. (This) could be to do with cages being something cheap and easy to experiment with as belts look too extreme. I'm into chastity but a full-on belt is just too "put upon" (for me).'

For another, the technical aspect came to mind, as did social changes, especially in the US: 'They are manufacturing way too many chastity devices for it not to have gained massively in popularity. I think much (of this) is to do with the changing roles of the sexes' he suggested, before adding that he thought a lot of women these days are into cuckolding their husbands, so that's not even 'kink' anymore. 'There isn't,' he continued, 'a college sorority girl who doesn't know what a chastity belt it, what a sissy is, what a bull is, what the spade means, what a "small" dick is and what a big dick is. Hell there was a song about not wanting a small dicked male. I see more and more teenage boys in drag at the malls being led around by their girlfriends. Times are a changing,' he concluded.

The ease of communication has also been identified and considered as an 'identifiable variable': 'The internet allowed fantasies and kinks to be published, read by a mass market for the first time and acted upon, so the popularity of BDSM equipment in general has increased since the mid-90s. Chastity devices are just one of many things being made, and sold on much larger scales than ever before', while one person suggested: 'I do not see it as evidence of any great socio-political change. BDSM stuff is consumed by all sexes and genders from all classes and wealth backgrounds, by those on all sides of the slashes. It is all booming right now. The internet has democratized BDSM, so any adult now can easily find out what it is about. So, logically, equipment and toys which are used in all our kinks and activities are out there and more than ever before.'

By 2015, numerous sites dealing with various aspects of chastity had appeared on the internet. Some have even been and gone, although formal academic research remains invisible. Perhaps this will change as attitudes to 'imaginative' sexuality and sexuality evolve and become less censorious. Ideas and opinions have become far easier to exchange and discuss. If they are archived, contributions to websites will provide an invaluable resource for the researchers of the future.

Psychology and perceptions

While this is presented primarily in the context of interaction between (gay) men, some aspects of the psychology of chastity may apply to circumstances involving men and women, although in these, the man is often be represented as the submissive in a power dynamic.

The terminology of SM or 'kink' is laden with paradoxes, historic connotations that are far from accurate and frequently misleading. SM comes from Sado-Masochism. Some equate this with violence; the interaction may be intense, even extreme, but is it violent if consentual? SM involves intense stimulation – which can be interpreted as pain. This is not the same as dominance and submission (D/s – where the power dynamic is represented by the upper case D and lower case s.) Here one person – again willingly – allows another to control them and influence their behavior(s). Bondage and Discipline (BD) is different incorporates aspects of both SM and D/s psychology. Additionally, Corporal Punishment (CP) involving beating, either spanking, caning, using a slipper or a paddle, or instruments such as sjamboks and whips may not be 'punishment' at all, but a pleasurable, if intense, route to an endorphin high.

Chastity seems to fall primarily within the realm of D/s – Dominance and submission – or, as it is increasingly known, 'power play'. Instead of one person having no choice in the dynamics of a relationship – for so long, for example, women were (and, in some cultures, still are) regarded as no more than chattels, or possessions. In the western world of the 21st century, control is willingly (consensually) abdicated by one person to another. A submissive should, in this context, *give* the control; it should not be *taken*. Someone who is submissive may not be subjugated, a term which carries connotations of compulsion. Similarly, a submissive may not be a slave. To add to the possible confusions, a t*op* may be sadistic, and get pleasure from seeing another enduring or enjoying intense discomfort or even pain, but not dominant. Conversely, a top may be dominant but not sadistic while a bottom may or not be masochistic and may or may not be submissive.

In many relationships, someone 'wears the trousers', not always in line with orthodox or conventional gender stereotypes within any culture or ethnicity. Male domination may be social and political while, simultaneously, domestic life may mirror a matriarchy. Situations where the 'leadership' is recognized and overt can be regarded as involving 'power *play*'. For some, the aspiration is Total

Power Exchange (TPE), except that such circumstances don't really involve any 'exchange' of power, but its transfer. If a relationship becomes established, the submissive may then agree to 'honor and obey' the dominant, but the genders and gender roles of each remain largely irrelevant. If a dominant woman wants to wear clothing that is regarded as the epitome of masculinity while a submissive man is dressed in attire that, for them, represents ultra-femininity, that is a visual (and tactile) manifestation of a psychological dynamic which, for others, is more subtle.

Play too is a convenient word. It can cover sex, sexual activity without penetration or activities that could be seen as SM or BD and involve CP. In cultures where reserve lingers, asking someone whether they want 'to play' may be more socially acceptable than asking them if they want to fuck.

Chastity – and power play – can extend the sexual dynamic and ambience from the sofa or the bedroom to more of life, a factor which may account for some of the growing popularity and openness.

Writing on the Lockedmen.net website, which he runs, 'Locked57' suggested that men want to experience chastity for a number of reasons. He cited control – as part of a more comprehensive power relationship, however long, and masturbation control. He also implied that guys may have more energy if they masturbate less, which reflects the attitude take by many athletes and sportsmen in the run-up to important contests.

Being horny does, of course, increase a guy's enthusiasm for sex. Within the context of kink play, being mentally horny or even physically aroused may provide the incentive a cowardly bottom may need so that the balance of desire rather than fear leans in favor of action.

At the most simple, a Dom may suggest that a bottom doesn't masturbate for a period of time – anything from a day or two to longer than a week – as a prelude to meeting and sexual activity. The combination of looking forward to the action together with the 'denial' can increase the fervor. For some, chastity 'play' is an extension of this.

Some men have reported – anecdotally – that fewer orgasms can mean more intense orgasms (along the lines of less is more), while others suggested that a period of denial in itself may increase the power (and pleasure) of an orgasm as quality over quantity.

As well as feeling 'relief' after ejaculation, some guys say they can be turned off for a while afterwards. One particular 'chastity friend' has reported that he suffers from serious 'downs' after he ejaculates; he feels as far from being turned on as it is possible to be and quite miserable. The mood should not, he said, be described as depression, but he admitted that he does feel lethargic and disinterested in much of life, for several hours, occasionally days, after he has had an ejaculatory orgasm. He added that he wants to put a distance between himself and his partner and experiences distaste for anything sexual. He so dislikes the mood swings that he would far rather not experience orgasm than have one. (Psychoanalysts may well enjoy speculating about the origins of such conditioning, but regardless of that, the effects for this particular guy are such that they provide a very real and powerful incentive for long-term chastity.)

Simply being locked can be sexually exciting for some guys. This may mean that the essential process of getting a device into place can be a challenge. Just as many men have to resort to particular psychological stratagems to be able to urinate in some circumstances, great imagination and self control may be required to provide a distraction that is sufficiently strong for an erection to subside and a cock ring, a sheath or a cage to be locked into place. For some, the relatively extreme physical tactic of plunging the genitals into a container of icy water may be the only recourse in such circumstances.

Within the culture of 'leathersex', the power differences between the Dominant and submissive – be they Master and slave or Top and bottom – may be emphasized by exaggerating the physical differences between the (older) Dom and (younger) submissive. In *The Leatherman's Handbook*, Larry Townsend recounted how this may be manifest in a requirement that the submissive should shave to become more boylike. The extent may be just the scrotum or the area around the genitals or more extensive, from head to toe, including the eyebrows and armpits. Similarly, locking away the cock may 'emasculate' a sub.

Chastity for others may represent the most pragmatic mechanism they have available for dealing with feelings towards their male genitalia that could, if more serious, be considered to be body dysmorphia, a dislike with their physical appearance. Psychologically, an individual's culture and upbringing may have led to unorthodox perceptions of gender or views that do not reflect the cultural mainstream of that locality and moment. For example, the concept of being the receptive partner in sex may be so firmly linked to womanhood that emasculation in some form or another may be the only practical route to being able to function sexually at all. Such individuals may not identify as transgender per se, but 'unmanly' – and chastity, while maintaining all other manifestations of masculinity such as some muscularity and body hair, may be a realistic alternative to surgical 'modification'.

More recently, readers of kink and other websites may well be aware of increasing references to '1950s' relationships' – probably best summarized in the concept that, in a rite publicly recording the relationship (also known as 'marriage') one partner agreed to 'honor and *obey*' the other. At that time in the cultural histories of North America and much of Europe, the obedient partner was a woman. Since then, attitudes have changed – but the concept of one partner swearing obedience to the other remains constant. In the 2000s, the assumption has become that, in a relationship between a man and a woman, the power dynamic will be neutral and equitable. However, while less public – and a quick internet search failed to disclose any recorded instances of a man publicly using the word 'obey' towards a woman in a marriage ceremony – such dynamics are more common than may, at first, be thought. Similarly, in the context of two gay men, the notion that one will obey, even submit, to the other has become far less covert as public attitudes towards homosexuality per se have become less censorious in many parts of the world.

The idea of wearing a ring as a symbol of commitment to another is far from new. For most, such bands are placed around a finger, often during a rite at which a public declaration of loyalty (and monogamous fidelity) is made. The formal registration of such relationships may, in some jurisdictions, automatically entitle those involved to inheritance and access rights. They may also be represented by (mutual) tattoos, piercings or wearing other items of 'jewellery' such as cockrings or ankle bracelets. Some may choose chastity devices.

(Similarly, in the age of technology, a Dom may consider calling on electronic devices to extend control or supervision of a submissive – from using GPS software installed on a cellphone that is permanently switched on to the use, with consent of course, of other monitoring applications. The sections on control and 'electro' in the alphabetic section of Part II cover this in greater detail.)

Again, upbringing and conditioning probably provide the strongest influences, but one partner may consider that the greatest 'gift' they can offer a partner is control of their sexual release. Alternatively, such control may be demanded. The depth of the emotion may be genuinely spiritual. Towards the end of the 19th century, the English poet Christina Rosetti wrote a Christmas carol in which a poor man asks what he can give, as he has neither the wisdom to 'do his part' or a lamb to offer. Instead, he concludes that all he can give is 'his heart'. The verse encapsulates the concept of 'giving one's all' to a figure whom one respects, admires and loves. Chastity can be a supremely intimate donation of oneself in this way.

For some, chastity is intrinsically linked to a relationship, while for others the power dynamic is almost irrelevant. They require a second person to provide the control that they would not be able to exercise over themselves. So, guys who like being locked may provide such mutual oversight for one another.

Similarly, the temptation to escape and stimulate the penis may decrease over time – the rationale being that as so much time has been spent locked, any 'release' would spoil that. Keyholders can, occasionally, overlook this aspect of the psychology. For example, unlocking for an hour or two to allow a guy who has been locked for several weeks to pass unhindered through airport security en route to meeting the keyholder may be subject to this reasoning or motivation – as the effort and experience would be spoiled or wasted if it was abused in this way.

Another factor that may be linked with chastity is that of the concepts of 'boy' and 'man'. Townsend's writing reflects a climate in the late 1960s and early 70s in which age appears synonymous with experience and experience – and that dominance is associated with increases in both. He records how shaving, especially of the pubic area, provides a reminder of Dom/sub interaction that lasts as long as it takes the hair to grow back – but also observes that the hairless 'boy' can be a very visual manifestation of a different role to that of the hirsute man. The 21st century has seen the emergence of 'clothed man/naked man' (CMNM) activity as yet another variation on this theme.

Similarly, such interaction can explore and enhance the trust between two people. The person whose body is being stimulated transfers or abdicates responsibility for making the decision about the moment at which damage may occur to the other, a choice which involves disproportionate confidence in that other person. Self-protection is, by its very nature, inherently cautious. The buzz can then be two-fold – from the psychological intimacy of the trust to the physiological beauty of the stimulation.

Someone may ascribe greater importance to the period for which consent is given, knowing full well and overtly, that some physical damage may occur. The threshold for many probably is, for example, that between bruising which may heal within a few days and breaking a bone. That person may know that they will have to deal with the 'pain' of an impact, perhaps to the point of screams, but the warmth of the bruising that follows is a sensation they relish and for which the discomfort of the process is acceptable and perhaps even exciting in itself. Damage, in BDSM and kink circumstances, should – of course – be considered in terms of mental as well as physical health.

One vital aspect of consent that both dominant and sub should remember is that, in all but the most extreme of situations, the sub retains the ability to 'vote with their feet'.

'Punishment' should therefore be an activity which does not bring pleasure. For someone who has consented to life within behavioral parameters agreed with, and enforced by, another, such activities may be physically and mentally challenging – such as repeatedly moving stones from one end of a yard to another, in a way that induces physical fatigue and mental boredom; the caning or other intense stimulation being saved for the delayed gratification and positivity of a reward, an approach that undermines the idea of motivators being carrots or sticks.

For some, the idea of being denied access to penile stimulation clearly is negative and a punishment while, for others, being kept locked for longer may be regarded as evidence that they are clearly succeeding in providing pleasure for a Dom.

Aspects of chastity – as with other dimensions of 'kink' – can sit uneasily against our perceptions of social norms and conventionality. This was summed up by a friend in the US. 'I am,' he said, 'conflicted. Generally, I live a "normal" straight, suburban family life and it just feels so weird to be locked in a chastity device at the family barbecue and occasions like that.' Despite being married and having children, and commuting from the suburbs by train every day to work in a city office, he added: 'I was meant for this. I feel that way in a meeting. I meant the other "suits" would be surprised and probably laugh their asses off at us if they spotted this thing at the urinal. But well, *family*, that's different. The business guys, it's none of their business.'

Probably, many of those guys may laugh, but they would simultaneously be intrigued and excited. They'd want to know what the device felt like, what affect it would or could have on them – psychologically and physically. They may laugh to defend themselves from others' speculation that they too might be 'weird' while simultaneously being turned on beyond measure – either at the thought of experiencing domination from another or at the challenge of relinquishing control over sexual release, and wondering how long they could each endure that.

This friend also – behind the façade of his suburban

conventionality – considers himself to be a masochist and gay. 'Going to the dentist for root canal work,' he said, 'reclined in the chair, with the CB in place but not showing, my dick would try to get hard.' He may claim to be a 'sick faggot', but this man's chosen identify is no sicker than many and, it could be argued that, by acknowledging and even exploring these aspects of his psyche, he is far less sick than those who try to repress such feelings.

Some 'alpha' guys may also appear to 'play' with submission. One dominant writing about control said of a submissive guy: 'I could sense his dom side beneath his stoic decision to be docile. I liked that tension' and his respect. For another, chastity is a manifestation of a life-long concern about having a small penis in a phallocentric world. His cock was, he revealed online, very sensitive and so, when he was seeking sex with rougher men, he focused on 'daddy dick' seeking anal penetration, adding: 'My young body was easily dominated and men took their pleasure from my tight hole .... Although that hurt, I felt it was my natural role ... Tops ... taught me that sex didn't need my cocklet and I learned that orgasms are cheapened by their abundance.

'I discovered the ability to cum through various stimuli,' he went on, 'I realized that manhood and manhood are separate and caging took me on a deep emotional journey and strengthened my sexual identity. I am,' he concluded, 'liberated in my sense of boyish masculinity and take pleasure in service ....'

Why?

Questions about the psychology appear online quite frequently. In April 2015, for example, one guy asked, on the Lockedmen website, whether anyone had done any *real* research to find out 'what drives us to want one of our most basic human male desires the ability to self-satisfy that demand to be kept from us'.

He also said that he knew that being horny was fun – but wanted to know what drives guys to want and *enjoy* this, before adding that he was similarly curious about other forms of BDSM from which he gained pleasure. 'There is nothing,' he said, 'in my childhood or adult life that I can remember that would drive this.'

However, he then went on to write that: 'Even at a very young age, say maybe three or four, I can remember running the bar of soap over my urethra to get that burning feeling, which I still do and enjoy very much.' He said he loved his penis, had no desire to cause it pain – but sought stronger, more intense sensations than sex or masturbation could provide.

The answers to his question were wide ranging – just as the comments on any of the (many) chastity websites reveal much about the various psychological perspectives.

In 2014, for a workshop in the United States, website owner Locked57 suggested that men seek cock control for several reasons – ranging from the constraint being just part of a broader power relationship to a means of reducing masturbation so that they had more energy and a greater desire for sex or SM play with others, to increase the quality of their orgasms, to maintain a level of horniness and arousal that would otherwise be dissipated by orgasm, as a sign of fidelity or commitment or, finally, as an indication of some sort of 'emasculation'

One guy said of being in chastity, 'you just have to forget about sex. It's not that bad.' Another said he was in chastity as surrender of control to a dom, giving the dominant 'one more thing to hang over my head' to ensure his behavior was line with the dominant's requirements. 'It is,' he said, 'about surrender and control for me. I am also a masochist who enjoys suffering for another's pleasure.' Suffering periods of being really horny provide enjoyment for the dominant, he added.

Another said he had been a slave for 25 years who had got his first device in the 90s as he 'loved the idea of being locked and owned', adding: 'It took a few years before Master took possession of the keys and refused to let me take the belt off.' It had, he continued, become 'everyday' rather than a fetish – and that he was turned on by having fewer rights than others, saying: 'I am naturally submissive and giving control over my sexuality makes me feel complete.'

A different contributor said that being locked gave him energy and focus – while a further submissive added that he also liked not having control as he wanted to please the top more, suck more and be used more – but did the 'why' really matter. (The answer to this is that – for those who have difficulty trying to rationalize behaviors and feelings that are perceived as 'unorthodox' in a world of conventionality – such information can help them accept themselves in that context. Others may have progressed or psychologically evolved to a point of acceptance and self-awareness – mindfulness even – where this not longer bothers them.)

Another suggested that it was 'an issue for hormonal balance, sexual release with human interaction and a longer recovery time from sexual release', prompting a further question asking whether chaste guys had more testosterone than others.

The effects of this – and 'orgasm cycle ups-and-downs' – were considered in more detail by a guy who locks himself. 'The feeling,' he wrote, 'of pent-up testosterone, that lust, that overflowing semen is like a drug in itself. When I'm so full of cum and can't release, it's as though it fills my body and intoxicates my heart and mind. In those lustful moments, I feel no fear and brim with confidence and inner strength,' – a power that others have described as being similar to 'roid rage'. However this guy added: 'I feel simultaneously manly and submissive; masculine and feminine'.

However, after release, he said that he 'crashes' into a state of being depressed and mentally weak, thinking immediately that he wants to 'raid the fridge and wallow in melancholy, listening to sad songs and filling my face with ice cream'. That feels, he added, like the 'male period'. He had, he explained, been through these revolving doors so often that now, even when deeply passionate, he doesn't dare race towards orgasm as he is frightened of what happens afterwards – 'the disappointment and regret that await' – with each making me ask myself 'did I have to do that? Couldn't I have enjoyed it just a little longer?' Anal milking, he added almost as an afterthought, did however make him feel alive and energetic.

The researchers behind a study, published in the journal *Psychoneuroendocrinology* in May 2003, said that they had found that, in many species, inhibition results from repeated ejaculations affecting receptors in the brain that control sexual behavior in rodents – but this line of investigation does not appear to have been followed up. A long exchange on the 'fap'- or abstinence from pornography – section of the reddit.com website that began in 2014 did cite this – but the discussion seemed more related to the 'testosterone hump' (described in more detail in Part III of this book) than any longer term effects on libido and sexual desire in men.

One man – with a female keyholder – said he had disliked his male genitals throughout his life until he discovered chastity. 'When I saw my first device,' he wrote, 'I knew I had to have one and be locked.' I was told I would have more energy – and found that to be true, he explained, adding: 'That energy amazes people who don't know I am in chastity and I am often asked where it comes from; I believe it may be something to do with the lack of orgasm cycle ups-and-downs.' His keyholder, he continued, likes both the energy and how the device 'protects me from abusing myself'. He also believed she liked the control. 'I didn't think she was listening to me in the beginning,' he wrote, 'so I over-pushed what I wanted and now she thinks I should maybe never orgasm again. I don't like never having orgasms, but I do like the energy and constantly being horny. It's like a perpetual sex high and I know that I am a very fortunate man who is completely at her mercy ...'.

This was endorsed by a man who said he had never put himself in chastity, having only been locked by an owner as a function of being that dominant's slave.

A further contributor was more scientific, suggesting that the answers would not be found until the brain was fully mapped; then, he suggested, (chastity) will be found to have multiple, different causes, 'not just nuances, but totally separate paths that overlap a little in the expression of chastity'. He offered some examples – from the guy who feels ashamed at sex and enjoys the lack of responsibility to the guy who 'gets off too easily and enjoys having to wait until the pressure and pleasure really build', then the bondage aficionado who needs a daily release, the guy who seeks the commitment of being 'completely tied and connected' to another (in the form of the keyholder) or even the feeling of safety emanating from having an 'armor-clad' dick in a dangerous world.

One dominant put forward a challenging approach: 'I never use physical devices on those that *need* them,' the dom wrote. 'My subs must show me they can be obedient and honor me with sexual obedience through their own self-discipline before I consider allowing them to have a device. That way, I always know they're submitting to me, not the device.' This dom added that the turn on came from a man 'choosing to do the right thing' rather than losing that control in a device. A sub contradicted this, saying that being locked was psychologically more powerful as it was a constant reminder of one's state. Another added: 'I feel that focusing on the dominant's needs and desires as much as necessary will do the trick. If the dominant wants the submissive to refrain from orgasm, that alone should be sufficient.'

Another considered chastity to be part of the 'BDSM spectrum' – without a single cause. He said he was not affected by money, status or materialism, the pursuit of happiness or progress in life represented by big cars, homes or luxury vacations. His focus was the 'warm contact between people, sharing thoughts and lives, making each other as happy as possible'. Spirituality and BDSM allowed some people he trusted to get into his soul while physically it means break through his own defences. 'Chastity,' he said, represented ways he could set his own goals, being more focused and increasing his horniness simultaneously as well as 'getting a deep dive into my soul and getting mentally touched'.

A different contributor added that chastity represented just one aspect of the control he had handed to a dominant – with others being his clothing and what he was allowed to eat and drink. This was followed by agreement that chastity was synonymous with submission and was more complex than simply finding a keyholder and the observation that one's own willpower gets boring, adding that: 'prolonging (the experience) for a dom, being submissive, leaving control to someone else, that goes so deep'.

One guy admitted trying self-locking without his partner's

knowledge but confessed that he was deterred by the inconvenience and discomfort. When the partner discovered the device and ordered its use, that was, he said, 'totally hot' but the partner then lost interest. After he became so interested again that he replaced the device, he came to the conclusion after 24 hours' wear that he needed a keyholder to 'make it seem worthwhile'.

Some tops lock too. In one online exchange, one bottom questioned the thinking behind this. If his Dom's cock was locked, he said, he would not be able to serve it. 'As a top,' he added, 'I would want to use my cock.' The first respondent said that, in his opinion, tops that were 'worth anything' would not put bottoms through experiences they have not tried for themselves. Another bottom said that his top said: 'My partner keeps me locked, but lets me out when he wants to ride me, then locks me again fairly regularly.'

One guy, who is both a top and bottom, added: 'If I wasn't kept locked between sessions, I'd be wanking all the time and having little or no interest and energy in playing with them (or other guys I keep locked).' He went on to explain that he might not cum while playing – very intensely – with his keyholder, as he could be too 'wiped out' to have any interest while he is only allowed to cum once a month with a regular locked guy, whom he sees a few times a week. Frustration was great, he said, when being sucked or edged, adding that: 'The situation feeds my top desires and my sub ones.'

One guy added that not having access to his cock did not prevent many types of 'play' either as top or bottom while another admitted to being a top that keeps his dick locked, adding: 'I'd love to get into a mutual key holding session with a boy.'

In a different exchange, a top said that (by locking) he was showing his own monogamous commitment to his submissive boy. The boy knew that just as the cock between his legs belonged to his dominant, the cock between his dominant's legs was exclusively his.

A more comprehensive and thoughtful response came from a guy who put forward the argument that for many, perhaps most, subs, 'there is the tacit assumption that if a guy is dominant he *ought* (his emphasis) to display his power through the medium of his cock and that he most certainly should *not* be interested in invading his own arse.' He then asked whether tops should be denied the 'extreme pleasure' of dildos, butt plugs, fists or sitting on the 'rock-hard cock of his tied-up sub' simply to try to meet the sub's, apparently misplaced, expectations. Isn't this, he suggested, control from the bottom up?

He explained that, as a top, his pleasure emanated from seeing the bottom excited by whatever was being done to or for him. 'If I cease to worry about which hole I am next going to poke ... and then transfer my concentration to the scene and the visible feedback from the guy I am controlling, I get all the pleasure I need. I don't have to end it abruptly just because I have shot a load. With the focus removed from my own cock, and knowing the terrific pleasure available by keeping it locked (in a secure metal cage), I choose to keep it locked, not cum in a scene – and the subs always come back for more.' Being a locked top was, for him, he said, 'a win-win situation'.

Similarly, the next contribution added that chaste tops had greater empathy with their bottoms and greater male bonding. They also, he added, were experienced and 'knew exactly what to do'.

Keyholding

Curiosity frequently surrounds the motivation of the Dom. Why does anyone want to lock someone else? What does that person get from it? One aspect may be as part of a wider power relationship or interaction in which control is important. Another person's chastity may not, in itself, have a great appeal, but as part of establishing and maintaining broader behavioral parameters, such as control, may enhance what else is happening.

Clearly when two people are together, one can get pleasure from touching the other and feeling the entrapped genitals. Being turned on more vicariously is another matter. Having an extra key on a bunch can be a reminder that a guy either across town or even across a continent or ocean is locked – and that you are thinking of him and his predicament, a reminder of the interaction that brings the two of you emotionally closer.

In sexual situations, a guy who is locked cannot play with his cock – so he has little alternative but to focus on alternatives, ideally the Dom. (The friend from whom I inherited my first Tollyboy belt could ejaculate while masturbating another man, especially if he was standing behind the guy. Even if he could not even get fully erect inside the penis tube, he would buck and thrust as if he was masturbating himself. He could, sometimes, even orgasm – and dribble ejaculated semen through the penis tube – at exactly the same moment as the guy he was touching. That was quite something to see and amazingly theatrical in its way. I also witnessed an occasion when the Dom stopped this, even though he was himself nearing orgasm. The Dom let my friend relax a little. He then instructed the friend to kneel and watch, hands clasped behind his back, as he masturbated himself to a climax. The ejaculate shot into my friend's mouth, but he was allowed no further stimulation after which he had, I was told, to wait for at least another couple of weeks before he was released from the device.)

Others find that without access to the cock, the sensitivity of the skin of the sac or their anus apparently increases, so enhancing their responsiveness if they are allowed to stimulate those areas themselves or the Dom does that for them.

From anecdotal comments, rather than empirical research, some men with smaller penises have developed anxieties about this and cultural norms of masculinity, 'performance' and the relationship between size and the ability to provide pleasurable stimulation for a partner during penetrative sex. Consequently, one guy said he found he had least 'performance anxiety' when the ability to perform was eliminated altogether. Another guy, whose penis is regarded as large by any standard, expressed almost entirely the opposite perspective; he felt he could potentially cause damage during penetration, so being locked relieved him of that anxiety.

Online research carried out for the Lockedmen website in 2014 attracted about 1,000 responses, although not every one of those individuals answered all the questions. The input from those who liked being locked revealed that more than 40 per cent – or 560 – of those contributing information said they liked the control and submission that went with being locked while 16 per cent, or nearly 90 respondents, said they liked being constantly horny. Of the keyholders, 70 per cent – or 93 respondents – said they enjoyed the power, control and being boss.

On a scale of one-to-five, more than a quarter said they were happy all the time they were locked. Three quarters of 380 respondents rated their happiness levels at '3', perhaps indicating that they were happy for about 60 per cent of the time. Fewer than a quarter – 155 respondents – put their scores at 3 or less.

Of nearly 400 guys who were locked when they answered the questions, more than 60 per cent (or 240 of them) said they enjoyed the feeling of being controlled while only one less said that 'it gets me excited'. About half – 180 respondents – said that being locked reduced their masturbation while a third said they were locked to stay horny for more general play while slightly fewer than a quarter said it was to stay horny for their partners. In terms of power dynamics, slightly fewer than a third – 111 or 20 per cent – said their chastity was part of a Dom/sub relationship while 20 per cent said their partners had demanded the chastity.

Fewer than a fifth of those answering – about 70 individuals or 18 per cent – said the locking was to help them achieve other goals, such as losing weight.

The question of who knows most about chastity is important too – and often overlooked. Guys who like being locked frequently have a more detailed knowledge of the devices available and which is most suitable and practical for them. Those who find themselves involved as keyholders may have less experience and expertise. Locked guys can use this information imbalance to their advantage – which is perhaps another reason why many like being locked by others 'on the receiving end' who may know some of the tricks used to try to elicit an early escape and can see through them very quickly.

As Locked57 wrote before a workshop at an event in the US in 2014, being a keyholder has advantages and disadvantages. From his long experience, he suggested that, as far as the responsibilities are concerned, the terms of the locking should be negotiated clearly before padlock snaps into place or a key is turned. The agreement or arrangement should cover all the *dimensions of consent* including the length of the locking period and other factors such as the device and what should be done in an emergency. Although talking about such 'terms' may be fun, verbal arrangements can easily – as in so much of life – easily lead to confusion. If you're together, then write down what you agree; if you're not, then exchange e-mails or other messages (which can then be printed) so that you both know exactly what commitments you are making to each other. For the guy who is locked, having a copy (or copies) of the document in view in particular places can be an exciting reminder of the predicament he has arranged for himself. For the keyholder, pleasure can be gleaned from knowing exactly what another guy is experiencing – or *not* experiencing – within the agreement.

Whatever the keyholder's enthusiasm, the terms of the arrangement do need to acknowledge the realities of a locked man's life. If he has others close by, such as family members or a partner who has other interests, then a large, ostentatious device may not be practical. If he needs to travel or enter public buildings with security arrangements that include metal detectors or fully body scanners, then allowing flexibility for short periods of unlocking for these occasions may also be sensible. (As is suggested elsewhere, using cameras on cell phones can be a useful – and relatively discreet – means of ensuring compliance in such circumstances.)

Regular contact is *very* important. Modern technology can be very helpful with this. If you're a keyholder, apart from the guy you have locked, and you suddenly think about him, whether you're driving along the freeway, walking round the supermarket, on the way to a business meeting or just after waking up in the morning, send him an electronic message saying just that. As a locked guy, knowing that a keyholder is enjoying the control is important – and such messages can not only be very reassuring but boost the enthusiasm of the lockee and, for those who are insecure, be emotionally powerful and important too.

Consent – across all the dimensions of who, what, where, when, how, perhaps even why, and how – is important as is being safe and sane. Safety and sanity (in case of emergencies) mean that, unless the keyholder can be guaranteed to be with the locked guy within 10 or 15 minutes should a crisis emerge, then the locked man should always have access to a key. Having them in key safes at home might seem like fun, but gaining access when time is of the essence may take longer than getting hold of the keyholder. Similarly, using a combination lock might seem a good idea – until the keyholder cannot be contacted.

Cutting the hasp of a small padlock is reasonably straightforward and most hospital emergency rooms have metal shears that will do that. Plastic tags can be cut very easily. However, breaking a device to allow release could be unnecessarily embarrassing – especially at a time of additional distress – and be extremely costly.

So what do you do? The most practical approach is for the lockee to have emergency access to a key or the combination necessary to unlock a device. Either can be kept very easily in a tamper-proof way – from a small envelope made additionally secure by a signature or other mark across the seal or in some sort of breakable locket. (Having a key that is effectively rendered unreachable on a necklace can add yet another psychological dimension to the experience – because the lockee will frequently be aware of its presence yet cannot do anything about the device between his legs. Every time he thinks about the key, he is reminded of his predicament.)

Quite a lot of men report being able to pull their penises out of various devices, yet far fewer seem capable of reinserting their cocks into cages or other tubes once they are out. Add-ons are – such as sharp polycarbonate points – can be attached to devices such as the CB series as a further deterrent, but once a cock is out and cannot be replaced, the 'freedom' is clearly visible to the keyholder. Evidence of when a cock had escaped may not be available, requiring honesty from a locked guy when reporting such occurrences, if the two are apart and meeting only occasionally – unless other monitoring measures are put into place.

For his workshop in 2014, Locked57 suggested that a top or dominant may want to lock others as part of a power dynamic, so the locked guy has more energy and interest in other play or sexual activity, simply as a service – because subs outnumber dominants, as punishment, a sign of commitment or fidelity, for self control and because they themselves find it sexually or emotionally pleasurable. The best way, he suggested, of achieving this is with a well-fitting, robust device that can be left in place for extended periods, that prevents ejaculation and by keeping the keys out of reach. He also recommended that (potential) keyholders should learn about chastity and chastity devices, and trying them on and wearing them for a while helps too, he said.

Is chastity an aspect of worship? The mindset of putting the dominant on a pedestal seems more prevalent in among those into 'femdom' interaction than among gay men (although this may only be a very personal observation). However, worship clearly has a place for many that is very closely aligned to being in chastity and locked.

Keyholder responsibilities

Being a keyholder incurs responsibilities, some of which are practical while others are psychological.

For one top, preventing a bottom from touching his cock during sex had one very simple but practical aspect, even though the locking might not last for long; it could, most fundamentally, prevent premature ejaculation. By this he meant preventing the sub's ejaculation before he was ready, rather than anything involuntary on behalf of the sub. He preferred reaching orgasm either at the same time as the sub or just before … rather than the sub climaxing too early.

For some subs, understanding the top's emotions can be difficult. The physical presence of a device is a perpetual reminder of one's predicament, however far away physically the keyholder may be at any particular moment. For the keyholder, relishing in the thought that another man – perhaps thousands of miles and several time zones away – cannot touch his penis and has to sit to urinate without making too much of a mess is more cerebral. The locked guy may think of the keyholder frequently – but keyholders have fewer physical incentives to think about those they have locked.

So, while those who are locked endure a regime of physical behavioral parameters, the obligations are more psychological or intellectual for keyholders. Locked guys can as easily become frustrated with keyholders as they can with their libidos, perhaps because the heightened emotional or hormonal effects may be associated with and targeted towards such individuals. Dealing with someone who is locked probably requires greater attention and sensitivity than 'merely' managing a 'pushy bottom'.

'Pushy bottoms'

Differentiating between 'pushy' and enthusiastic may not be easy for a top either, especially when chastity adds – relatively quickly and also over time – to the psychological state of someone who is locked. From personal experience and observation, someone who has been in chastity for a period of time may become more emotionally exposed, with an increasing propensity either to talk about sensitive and very personal topics in ways which may challenge social conventions or by becoming more sensitive themselves and more likely to display mood swings of a greater amplitude than usual and more often. Emotional exposure is not the same as vulnerability. The reaction to a challenge or threat may be 'passive aggressive' and like that of the spoiled child rather than a collapse into tears. The keyholder – whether they are living with the lockee or exercising control at a distance – needs to be aware of these heightened and more exposed emotions. After that, appreciating the need to provide and maintain contact that will not evoke an inappropriate and unwanted negative reaction becomes important.

In early 2015, a spat erupted on one website because a post included the words 'a keyholder *should*' (my italics). One respondent – the nickname indicated an American woman – just commented 'gotta love guys who are full of ... should'. Another said keyholders should do whatever they please, 'not what a chastity sub thinks they should do'. A third was more analytical: 'If my keyholder doesn't do all the things I can think about to prove they have the power, they aren't doing it right and can't be considered a true keyholder. After all, they have the key so they have the responsibility to leverage it. I'm giving up my penis; they have to make it worth my while, right?'

Perhaps the best way to resolve this perpetually thorny dilemma is to suggest that the word *could* replaces *should*.

Also, confusion can quickly appear when expectations have not been identified and assessed. Frequently, pushy bottoms challenge tops to try to elicit further information about their feelings and expectations. Equally often, anecdotal evidence indicates that bottoms do more to try to analyze their own emotions and psyches than tops – so self- and mutual awareness is imbalanced. Taking time to communicate – perhaps using the 'dimensions of consent' as a starting point – may well also reduce any need a bottom may find himself feeling to be pushy and give the keyholder greater information about the sub which can (over time) be explored for the satisfaction and excitement of both.

This then becomes, as much as anything, an exercise in managing expectations. Those who are locked can also behave contrarily; they may bleat and beg to be unlocked but, immediately the keyholder succumbs, they resent the collapse of the domination. Pre-locking negotiation must, therefore, be extremely comprehensive; each and every aspect should be discussed, perhaps several times, and the agreements documented and acknowledged by each. (Unlike negotiation zillion-dollar international trade deals, where the main possible loss for the principal parties involved is financial, the fall-out from the combination of the emotional and sexual, even for one person, can – and probably will be – more than disproportionately painful as far as any disappointment is concerned.)

Once the terms have been agreed, the onus is on both the keyholder and the person being locked to uphold that agreement. The keyholder may, to repeat, be perceived as sacrificing all credibility as a dominant if unlocking is allowed too early (without, for example, appropriate logistical reasons). From the opposite perspective, the locked person may lose that keyholder by failing to fulfill the contract.

Returning to the psychological, the keyholder similarly should establish and maintain regular contact with the person who is locked. Additionally, extra contact can really boost someone who is locked.

Some suggestions have come from those with female domination ('femdom') interests, but the emotions seem not to be gender specific at all. One dominant wrote online of 'letting subs come plenty' – but at the dominant's whim: 'when I want, how I want and where I want'. For me, that person added, 'chastity is about control' and that being in charge of the boyfriend's orgasms was symbolic of the ownership of him.

That dom then went on to give examples of the rules they had put in place. He was, for example, only allowed to masturbate to ejaculation while kneeling on the floor or lying on his back if he was being penetrated anally. Whether or not they were together, he was only allowed to reach orgasm with permission. He had to ask using specific words. The dominant could then say no, command him to 'edge' for different lengths of time or grant permission if he obeyed further instructions. He could face having to cum within a (very short) period of time, perhaps seconds rather than minutes, or perform other (humiliating) tasks. If he failed, he faced extra restrictions and perhaps even punishment.

This dominant also said that 'the myth of chastity being denial fuels the misconception that dom(mes) only want to torture and cuckold their subs and don't want overt sexual contact with them'. That dominant admitted to being a sadist, but added that the turn-on came from consensual intensity.

'Torturing my sub until he's a bloody, crying mess makes me want to climb onto his face and grind against his tongue,' the dom wrote. 'It makes me want to hold him down and fuck him in the ass. It makes me want to suck his dick. It makes me want him in all ways. Knowing that I own him so completely that he can't even complete a basic human function without my permission only heightens my desire for him. So, while savoring every orgasm he gives me while he's in chastity makes them that much sweeter, but finally granting him permission to cum and watching him writhe in ecstasy is possibly more satisfying.'

One dominant sad that while 'deeply sexy', chastity is far more than that – and an expression of love 'It is,' the keyholder wrote, 'a tangible way to manifest my ownership of my sub and his surrendering of control and devotion to me.' Being asked to keyhold by strangers was, said this dom, 'repulsive' as pledging commitment to someone you had never met was, as far as he was concerned, 'inconceivable'. Chastity, the writer continued, not only heightens the intensity of every orgasm, it imbues each with meaning. Each orgasm granted becomes beautiful as a gift from dom to sub and from sub to dom, adding: 'Chastity turns what is usually a self-indulgent act into an offering, not just of the body, but of the soul', requiring great trust (that the sub won't cheap and that the dom will not push the sub so far that abuse occurs).

Chastity also requires great trust – that the sub won't cheat and that the dom will not abuse the trust, or push the sub beyond his limits. We need to communicate, said his dom, so a sub can tell me if restrictions are not OK, adding: 'If someone isn't capable of communicating with me … we're done.'

One response to this agreed that chastity was not about 'denial' but 'restriction', comparing his relationship to that of a pet tiger. 'I want,' he said, ' a relationship with someone who loves, admires and respects me but desires and requires physical control for our mutual benefit, which should extend to both pain and pleasure to be complete. Orgasm control without any orgasms or sex misses the point.'

Again and again, comments have been posted that chastity not only increases the intensity of orgasm but imbues each with meaning. 'When you discard the baggage associated with chastity in porn and get down to it,' said another, 'it's an incredibly and connected type of power exchange.' Another dominant added: 'Someone allowing me complete control of their genitals is a gift which I don't take lightly.'

A fundamental doubt expressed by many men regards self control. Some say they don't need chastity – because they can obey instructions. Others like devices as symbols of submission and a dominant's desire for ownership and submission, in addition to words of agreement and respect. Others, who say they don't *need* locking, feel that devices add new levels of fun to their relationships, increasing horniness and submissiveness simultaneously.

One dominant said online that chastity was about trust and deeply caring for one another – with the submissive saying: 'I freely give this power over me to you' while another man said chastity helped him focus on 'feminine' thoughts and feelings (whatever those may be to him) and stopped male thoughts 'clogging' his emotions.

Another said he found it easier to control his urges when locked, but the constant pressure was a constant reminder of the one he served. A further guy said he had been 'selfish' with his orgasms and had had trouble 'submitting as a primal man' but that being locked created a duality that allowed him to be controlled easily while yet another said his device was 'mostly for adornment'.

Later, a different guy said: 'I don't serve. I like to obey or be given no further option which, to me, is fundamentally different'. He did, he said, like wearing a reminder of being owned and obedient, not unlike a collar and leash. But, he added, 'it would be completely useless if I wasn't allowed regular release; there would be no motivation.'

Gender perceptions are also repeatedly challenged in discussions of the psychology of chastity. One online question asked, simply: 'Is your penis the only thing you have that defines you as a man?'

Perhaps this was self-justification, but another man wrote: 'Yes, I can serve my dominant, but I am not a service slave or bottom. Doing chores … is not my favorite. I do them willingly in exchange for what the dom does. If we did not do the kinky things we do and have the dynamic we have, we would split the chores. It is a way to show my gratitude, so I serve relentlessly.'

A locked man wrote that he could still be a protector and provider, but they alone did not define his masculinity; that, he said, was a role he played in society. 'If given the choice, I would be a puppy,' he added, but puppies don't pay the bills ….

Perceptions

Online research carried out for the Lockedmen website in 2014 attracted slightly more than 1,000 responses – providing an informal overview of (primarily) gay male internet users with an interest in chastity. Of the respondents, 70 per cent identified themselves as gay, although another 20 per cent claimed to be bisexual. Nearly 10 per cent said they were straight while 0.6 per cent identified themselves as celibate and 0.9 per cent as asexual.

Slightly more than a quarter were aged between 26 and 35, with 20 per cent aged between 16 and 25. Another 19 per cent were aged between 36 and 45 while 20 per cent were between 46 and 55 and 11.5 per cent were in the 56-65 age bracket. The remaining 4 per cent were older than 66.

Most – 55 per cent – said they were single while 30 per cent were in relationships and living together while 15 per cent were partnered but living apart. More than three-quarters – 76 per cent – said their partners were male, but 24 per cent of those who answered this question, had female partners. (Fewer responses were received to this question than the entire survey, so this may not be unduly different from the breakdown between those claiming to be gay or bi.)

A significant majority – slightly more than 70 per cent – said they were currently having sex while 25 per cent said that this had stopped and 5 per cent said they never had.

The interest in chastity had – for nearly 80 per cent – lasted for a few years or longer, while 12 per cent said it had appeared within the previous couple of years. Just 3 per cent, or 30 respondents, said their interest had begun within the previous month.

The huge majority – only just less than 90 per cent or more than 900 respondents – reported that they had been locked during the previous 12 months. Nearly 25 per cent – or nearly 250 people – had also been keyholders. Only 6 per cent had had no chastity experienced during the preceding year. Of those 60 respondents, more than 60 per cent said they didn't know a suitable potential keyholder while slightly more than 50 per cent also said they did not their own devices. Of these respondents, 22 per cent said they didn't know anyone who they could lock and 35 per cent said that their current life or relationships made locking difficult.

The role of the internet was reinforced – with 50 per cent saying that they had held keys for online friends in the previous 12 months. Regular 'playmates' and partners together accounted for nearly 36 per cent of those being locked while 33 per cent were in-person friends and 32 per cent were considered to be slaves, subs or boys. Casual playmates accounted for 27 per cent of those being locked.

Most locking was reported to be for relatively short periods – with about 25 per cent being for a week or less and another 25 per cent being for a 'few weeks'. Another 12 per cent of the respondents said they had kept other locked for a month while 16 per cent had been locked for between two and three months. A further 30 per cent had been locked for periods from four to six months to between six months and a year. Another 9 per cent were reported to have been kept locked for between 12 and 24 months – 6 per cent – or for longer, 3 per cent.

Being locked did not seem to prevent other activities – with 44 per cent saying that they had engaged in BDSM activities in person with someone who was locked while 43 had told their guys they had been locked to be naked and about the same number had been instructed to shave (parts of) their bodies. Nearly 40 per cent had been involved in activities perceived as humiliating while about the same number had been 'edged' in person or been told what to wear. About 30 per cent had been allowed to ejaculate or achieve orgasm in the presence of the keyholder while between 20 and 23 per cent had been involved in activities using internet video facilities.

The research also revealed – or confirmed informal suspicions – that most guys, more than three-quarters or 78 per cent, were locked in 'genuine' polycarbonate CB devices while nearly 30 per cent more were in the silicon Birdlocked or Bon4 designs. Nearly 20 per cent had been locked in Mature Metal devices while another 20 per cent were in metal devices that had been manufactured in China. Another 17 per cent of guys had been locked in Holy Trainer designs while only about 15 per cent were in 'full' metal belts – of whom 9 per cent, or 22 men, were in Goethals or Carrara belts and 16 – or 6 per cent – were in Neosteel produced. Another 14 guys, or 6 per cent, had been locked in other full belts. Nearly 15 per cent – or 35 guys – were in devices made by Steelworxx in Germany. The keyholders also reported that 13 per cent of the guys they had locked were in metal cages made in the US while another 10 per cent, or 23 men, were in Chinese-made plastic devices. 'Other devices' were worn by 9.5 per cent or 23 locked guys.

Nearly half – 47 per cent – of those answering from the perspective of keyholders said they liked the role and had introduced chastity into an existing friendship or relationships. About 45 per cent said they primarily looked for guys to lock and that any play or other sexual activity followed from that. Nearly 40 per cent said they were usually approached by men looking for keyholders while 20 said chastity had been suggested by a sub with whom they were already playing.

More than 80 per cent said they enjoyed the feeling of control when they were keyholding while more than three-quarters also reported that locking guys 'gets me excited'. More than half – 53 per cent – said they did it to keep someone horny for playing with them while slightly fewer – 46 per cent – said the locking was part of a Dom/sub relationship. Slightly more than a third – 38 per cent – said they held keys as a service or to help others while nearly 10 per cent demanded locking of their partners.

As Lockedmen is a site aimed at men, many of whom identify as gay, the finding that 94 per cent of those answering the 2014 questions said their keyholders were other men while just 13 per cent had female keyholders is consistent with a number of the respondents being bisexual rather than exclusively gay.

Just over half those answering as locked guys said they were locked for periods of less than two weeks, while 16 per cent went for two-to-three month periods and another 13 per cent went for periods of about a month. Longer locking was less common – with about 7 per cent going for between four and six months while only a few more than 6 per cent (or about 60 respondents) went for between six months and a year. Only 34 respondents – 4 per cent – said they had been locked for between one year and two while only 2.5 per cent, or 25 respondents, said they had been locked for longer than two years.

While 19 per cent reported experiencing a month, about 16 per cent said they had never been locked for longer than a week. Another 18 per cent said they had gone between two and three months while 6 per cent had not 'cum' for between four and six months. Another 6 per cent said they had not cum for between six months and a year while less than 4 per cent, or 37 respondents, had gone for longer than a year.

Locked respondents also reported that they had regularly engaged in other activities with their keyholders – ranging from shaving body hair (45 per cent) to being naked when ordered (43 per cent) or having BDSM sex in person (41 per cent). Other activities included being instructed to wear specific clothing (33 per cent), 'humiliation' of some sort (31 per cent) or being allowed to cum with the keyholder watching or present (30 per cent). Slightly less frequently occurring were being edged in person or on cam or BDSM activity monitored using internet cameras. Additionally, 11 per cent said they had been permitted to cum without their keyholders present while 17.5 per cent said they had had vanilla sex while locked.

For some guys, sleeping in a chastity device can be difficult. Perhaps surprisingly, only six of those taking part in the Lockedmen website online research in 2014 reported this – while 13 said that chafing and soreness made them unhappy about being locked.

What does this all tell us? For a start, many locked guys seemed very willing to answer the questions and, even if the sample wasn't scientifically chosen, it is relatively large. The responses also reveal that chastity is, for many, a component of relationships or accompanies other activities. The survey additionally confirmed that, for such guys, the practice represents a very important and significant part of their lives. Another reality, corroborated here, is that the question of who is 'pleasuring' whom is at the core of much chastity play.

As anecdotes have already revealed, for some, the need to transfer pleasure to another, the object of their desire is all-important. For example, in 2014, one contributor to the Fetlife website wrote: 'I feel the need to crave the desire to serve a Dominant as I am being teased and denied mercilessly for days on end. It's the feeling of being controlled body, mind and soul that shortens my breath and gets the adrenaline running.'

This writer adds that the hypnotizing state you get in when your mind is taken over means that there is very little that you will not do to satisfy the other's desires. Being naked at the feet of the dominant and providing repeated orgasms, looking deeply into the dominant's eyes and seeing a smile of pleasure – and being told 'that was amazing my slave, but you don't get any release tonight ...' evoked deeper ecstacy. 'I will tremble at those words,' the writer continued, 'but understand that I must continue to work harder and continue to serve in order to earn my release' but only at the Dominant's discretion. 'I love to be teased mercilessly and denied; this only increases my desire and need to serve. Tease me and keep me on edge and there is very little I won't do. I love to go to sleep at night knowing that my (dominant) has been completely satisfied while I lay there denied, frustrated, horny, and completely submissive in a loving embrace.'

This contributor went on to explain that, for him, this provided a 'powerful feeling of freedom and release from the everyday control and dominance I have in my Alpha male world'. He was, he said, 'a dominant business owner by day and a submissive naked slave to a beautiful Dominant by night.'

Does it matter that he ended by confessing that: 'This is my fantasy'? In these circumstances, probably not – because the importance is the psychological strength of the need to abdicate the obligations and responsibilities of nine-to-five workaday existence by finding a freedom in transferring so much decision-making to another. Paradoxically, like so much in the realm of dom-sub interaction, the desire could also be regarded as simultaneously being extremely selfish.

Similarly, the gender of the dominant, the focus of this man's desires, is irrelevant. Although, in this anecdote, a male expresses heterosexual desires, the emotional craving could equally be from a homosexual man towards another male. Additionally, I have encountered a gay man who, for whatever deep reasoning and conditioning, felt that his 'place' was as the submissive to a woman – because that was how he perceived his own 'worth' or value. Such a manifestation of an individual's self-esteem may represent cause for concern about this as a mental health indicator. While such complex psychological conditioning may be more appropriately considered elsewhere, it remains a reminder that both physical chastity and desires for chastity control may be very deep-rooted and exceedingly convoluted.

The psychology can vary of course. One posting on Fetlife, challenging 'predatory' women seeking men to dominate came from a man who said he tended 'compulsively' to challenge consensus attitudes 'usually for the worse and occasionally for the better', by asking whether any men considered chastity to be a 'vanity choice'. He suggested that, after millennia of societal modesty, women – or at least some women – appeared to be seeking gender validity as hunters in their own role, an aspect of liberation.

Is it possible, the guy asked, looking to the converse of this, 'that some men see chastity and restraint as positive? Even perhaps, immensely attractive and self-affirming? Is it possible for a man actually to feel a little vain about the being chaste, chastised and 'inaccessible'?

The first respondent said that while his keyholder (a woman) felt that keeping him in chastity was a measure of control, he added that 'for me it's a measure of devotion ... and vanity doesn't enter into it.' Another said he had given himself to his partner, so that chastity had become an important aspect of the power and ownership, 'essential a symbol' of total control and makes everything perfect in the respective roles. 'For myself,' he added, 'I love it because it literally takes my manhood away – which, again, is perfect for my role and how I feel inside.'

This 'vanity' approach to chastity appears psychologically rational – based on the argument that someone is mentally strong enough to exist, even thrive, without sexual release or the need for genital contact. Having greater priorities than sexual release may also be rationalized as could taking pride in this apparent 'superiority' of mind over cock, a notion that is comparable to the individual who takes pride in service rather than humiliation. Submissives who have sufficient self-esteem to, for example, kiss the feet of a dom in public demonstrate a confidence that allows them to perform such tasks or rituals without concern for the attitudes of others. Some may perceive such confidence as verging on arrogance or smugness, while others remain challenged by the inner battle between their own desires and societal norms or conventionality. The question evolves, therefore, from being whether this form of restriction is a manifestation of confidence or whether the self-justification and presentation of the predicament in a positive way could be camouflaging other, less positive, emotions.

One dominant, again contributing to the Fetlife website, admitted letting subs ejaculate – but when, how was at the dominant's discretion. 'For me,' the writer continued, 'chastity is about control', adding: 'Owning my boyfriend's orgasm is symbolic of my ownership of him, so we have rules in place that dictate the nature of his/my orgasms.' The writer then goes on to recount how ejaculation may only be permitted by masturbation (rather than during penetration), in positions that are uncomfortable and strain other muscles and controlling the approach of the ejaculation while simultaneously begging for permission and not knowing whether it will be granted. The sub may be challenged to agree how many days will pass before another orgasm may be earned or endure other 'tortures' or deprivation.

This particular keyholder went on to repeat the increasingly widely held view from 'serious and experienced practitioners' that the 'myth' of chastity linked to denial 'fuels the misconception that Dommes only want to torture and cuckold their subs' without overt sexual contact. While she says she is 'sadistic' and enjoys intense physical and mental stimulation, she also says that putting a submissive guy through such sensations 'makes me want him in all ways', adding: 'Knowing that I own him so completely that he cannot even complete a basic human function without my permission only heightens my desire for him.' While she enjoys her orgasms while the guy is locked, 'finally granting him permission to come and watching him writhe in ecstasy is possibly more satisfying,' she writes. (The concept of cuckolding seems more prevalent where the dominant is a woman rather than a man.)

The same writer also considers – probably like many – that chastity can be an expression of love, a 'tangible way to manifest my ownership of my sub and his surrendering of control and devotion to me'. Consequently, keyholding casually for those she does not know cannot reflect this particular dynamic and does not appeal. Chastity 'imbues each orgasm with meaning' – becoming a mutual gift between those involved. Such emotions can be regarded as reflecting the vows of a relationship where one of those involved agrees, pledges and is excited (psychologically and sexually) to 'honor and obey' the other. Alternatively, the 'mutual gift' can be prepared to the spark between the fingers not unlike that depicted by Michelangelo in the section of his decoration of the ceiling of the Sistine Chapel in Rome that presents the creation of Adam.

The power of chastity was evident in a long Fetlife posting from a guy who had been locked for most of a decade. That, he claimed – probably rightly – allowed him to speak with as much authority on the subject as anyone, so he did, defining what he considered to be nine 'truths' about chastity.

The first, he argued, was that the only truly secure device was the mind, because he explained 'there are only various levels of difficult to obtaining an orgasm' – but that, more specifically, the security came from the relationship with a dominant partner.

The second was commitment. Chastity, he contended, was 'not a game' so that the third truth was that the penis no longer belonged to the body to which it was attached but to the dominant. 'That's right,' he wrote, 'it's not your cock anymore. You sold it. Contracted it out. Gave it away.' Once you have a partner who is a keyholder, then the fantasies and the game are over. A guy might have to piss sitting down or over his balls, but that is part of the deal. Cheating is betraying that partner – and the consequence may be, rightful, anger, he said.

A chastity device should be regarded as a wedding band, this man said, as truth five, so that – truth four – a comfortable device was essential because you're going to be in it for a long time, regardless of what you're doing.

That, he said, as truth six, was 'hot'. When the time comes for sex, he continued, 'you're going to turn into that wanton whore that will have you going after everything and everything'. The lust is nothing if not powerful. 'Am I a slut?' he asked, before answering: 'Absolutely. Why? Because I'm desperate. I don't have a cock any more, I have a mouth and an ass and I want to be fucked in both. Oh, but I can't cum. I want to. I'm obsessed with it.' He said he could almost get there, but never achieve orgasm. He would be swollen, dribbling and making a mess and 'miserable', his legs giving out before his lust. 'When it's over, and you feel like jelly, you'll thank your partner,' he said, 'and be just as randy and ready for the next person.' This is, he added, what the owner has done. They have created a monster that is insatiable.

The seventh truth, this man advocated, is 'you'll adapt'. Everything that irks and prompts complaints will go away, whether that's the sleeplessness, the erections, the chafing or the rubbing. Adjustments will, he said, become second nature and you will no longer feel uncomfortable – and 'you'll stop getting hard every time you look at something that turns you on.'

His eighth truth is that 'you're helpless'. He suggests that the dom – in his situation another guy – still needs to know how to 'push your buttons'. 'And,' he added, 'if they want to see (your) cock hot and bothered, you can't stop them.' That is why, he said, they hold the key. It's (about) power and control. They (the dominant), he said, will adapt too, and find ways to make you regret handing over the key. The dominant will remind the locked guy that he once thought chastity was a game, one he used to play for himself, as part of the teasing you when he wants to be unlocked. The lookee will be reminded of the pleasure that originated in a cock in the past, suggesting that he may be excited by such memories, further adding to the torment.

His ninth truth is, for some, what has attracted them to chastity in the first place – a hatred of orgasms. This reconditioning can be achieved in other aspects of the psyche – from learning to visualize cigarettes for example as sticky tube of disease-causing tar – or seeing cheese as lumps of fat, clogging arteries. Men's bodies can, this man suggests, can become so accustomed to not ejaculating that the muscles atrophy and orgasms become painful. Ruined orgasms can be mentally debilitating, eliciting tears or anger or even laughter. This man emphasized the physical unpleasantness that can result after sufficient (re-)conditioning while others report that 'post-orgasmic depression', especially if it lasts, is what motivates them to be in chastity.

Comments provoked by this included one which further stressed the addition of control to a relationship – in a way which was manifest in a chastity device. Another agreed that a relationship involving chastity was about the psychology and loyalty. Others found happiness in confirmation, either for reasons of gender or body dysphoria, in relinquishing control of, or access to, the penis. As these suggest, the divide between the glorious and the negative can be very narrow and nuanced.

The paradox of power and submission has long been identified. Writing in *Entertainment for a Master*, published in 1986, John Preston mentioned 'those men who need to have some balance in their lives'. He went on to add (of one man): 'I knew the story. I had heard it a million times. The man in charge, the one in control .... (He was) everyone's ideal of the American male. He was decisive in business, a leader in small groups .... For him, there was no escape. The dirty little secrets of his adolescence had terrified him and sent him scurrying into a deep and forbidden cave where they were made safe.' That man was symbolic of those who need someone else to take charge, 'to relieve you of the pressure of decisions ... of responsibilities.'

This was reflected in an online posting in late 2014. Chastity 'is,' one man wrote, 'a powerful feeling of freedom and release from the everyday control and dominance I have in my alpha male world.' His fantasy was, he added, to be 'a dominant business owner by day; a submissive naked slave by night.' His drive was strong. 'I feel', he wrote, 'the need and crave the desire to serve a dominant ... as I am being teased and denied mercilessly for days. It's the feeling of being controlled, in body, mind and soul that shortens my breath and gets the adrenaline flowing.'

He described how he achieved a hypnotic state when his mind was controlled by a dominant, whose desires he would do almost anything to satisfy. 'To me, there is nothing more exciting to be naked at the feet of my dominant, looking after every need and desire, working for complete satisfaction, from orgasm to orgasm, looking deep into the other's eyes to be told "that was amazing, my slave, but you don't get any release tonight".'

He would, he continued, tremble at those words, but continue to serve and work harder to earn release at the dominant's discretion, further increasing those needs. 'I love,' he said, 'going to sleep knowing that my dominant has been satisfied while I lie denied, frustrated, horny and completely submissive in love.'

Locked tops

As in so much of life, the roles assumed in chastity are not always fixed. The idea may, at first, seem paradoxical. However, some (male) tops get locked too.

One exchange discussing this was started by a guy who said that, as a top, he would want to use his cock. The responses reflected the great diversity of those with chastity interests. One said succinctly that 'any top that's worth anything won't put a bottom through anything they haven't tried himself' while another pointed out, equally pertinently, that 'top does not always mean dominant'.

Another man revealed that: 'I'm both top and bottom (for penetration), but I'm almost always in a submissive role. My partner keeps me locked up, lets me out when he wants to ride me, then locks me again fairly regularly.' A third confessed that: 'If I wasn't kept locked between play sessions, I would be (masturbating) all the time and have no energy or interest.' He admitted to having desires as both top and bottom. He did not always orgasm after intense (SM) play with his keyholder but a guy he kept locked was frustrated at only being allowed to bring him to orgasm once a month, even thought they 'played' far more frequently. It was, he said, a 'win-win' situation.

Someone else posted that: 'I like the frustration of not having access to my cock; it doesn't prevent many types of (SM) play either as Dom or sub.' A locked top said he would like to get into a mutual keyholding arrangement with a sub while a more thoughtful contribution suggested that: '… for many (probably the majority of subs), there is the tacit assumption that if a guy is a top/dom, then he *ought* to be displaying his power over his sub through the medium of his cock, and that he most certainly should *not* be interested in invading the interior of his own arse.' He went to on ask why, adding: 'Is a top to be denied the extreme pleasure of the dildo, the butt plug, or even the fist, or to sit himself down on the rock hard cock of his own tied-up sub, just to keep up appearances to match the expectations of the sub who thinks it just isn't top-like?' Is this, he wondered, possibly control from the bottom? 'For me,' this guy continued, 'as a top, my focus is on the sub, and so long as he is getting excited by whatever I am doing to or for him, then I am getting my pleasure out of it too.'

The intellectual dimension of this provides the buzz for some – as they revel in the apparent (further) contradiction of sexual norms in so many societies. For others, relatively simple practicalities and realities add to the delights.

One locked top says that he decided long ago that he preferred the quality of occasional orgasms to the quantity of the many, poor ones he would 'experience' rather than enjoy if he was unlocked and perpetually masturbating. He also says that if he's locked while playing with another man sexually, the focus changes from his cock to a far greater 'whole body' experience. We forget, he says, that the skin is the biggest organ of the body – and we waste so much of it by ignoring the opportunities for stimulation that it offers.

(Clearly, for those who are uneasy with their own body image or some body shapes this may present a further challenge. However, the mechanics of nerve endings and sensual simulation are the same regardless of whether a guy is a 'big man' or a muscled Adonis with minimal body fat. The anatomical and physiological glories of such arousal can be infinitely greater than the visual aesthetics, once that cultural conditioning can be overcome.)

This top has an arrangement with a guy he keeps locked that he only has one ejaculatory orgasm a month, regardless of the sexual activity. If he finds himself approaching orgasm, he has to stop and 'calm down'. Sex is no longer mechanical, a ninety-second whizz-bang that leaves no one really satisfied. The locked bottom can find himself being used for hours, little by little, during this mutual challenge.

The same locked top has an arrangement with his locked guy that he is only allowed to cum once a month – and that is only when the locked guy is top. 'If,' he adds, 'the top cums or the top causes the sub to have a second orgasm that month then the top gets punished – usually with some strokes on the top of the thighs with an implement of the punisher's choice.' However, this locked top does allow himself the freedom of being unlocked when he plays with this particular lockee.

Rules, he says, have to be negotiated and agreed – and then observed. Those two processes can add to the fun too. The locked guy may see his role as assisting the top to achieve orgasm – and accepting that this is not going to happen very often may challenge his perceptions too. However, that doesn't mean that he is not going to get a lot of attention or a lot of stimulation. Indeed, with both potentially increasing their horniness levels through locking, they may actually spend far more time intimately stimulating one another than would otherwise be the situation.

The other aspect of this involves the top compromising – or adjusting – his scope for control, so he can't simply say to the locked bottom 'I'm feeing horny, give me the key, boy'. Total honesty does help – as does the acceptance of sanctions of some sort if the deal is broken, or the top tries to break the rule. The mutuality of the pledge in this situation genuinely must be sacrosanct. In such circumstances, arrangements have to be made which prevent the boy from obeying this particular instruction. It may be that, when the top's arousal is predictable – during play, for example – the keys are out of reach in a safe with a time lock that cannot be overridden. At other times, balancing this particular sort of deprivation with emergency access requirements will need greater thought.

For another two guys in the US, the top's commitment to his locked 'boy' is to give the boy the key to his cock. This boy is allowed to unlock the top whenever he wants cock – but the deal is that he has to bring the top to ejaculatory orgasm. That may seem straightforward enough, but if the top is tired or 'over-drained', that may not be possible. Many men can become erect and stay that way for quite long periods of time when they're being aroused, but they may nevertheless not ejaculate or achieve orgasm. If the bottom chooses one of these times, under their arrangement, he will be punished. So, he had to learn to 'read' his master/top, to know when he was likely to want sex that would lead to an ejaculatory orgasm.

So, what do we glean from all this? Certainly, that the desires that drive a man towards liking either the idea or the reality of being in chastity, be that through self-control or using a device, are numerous and hugely diverse. The consensus appears to be that this is not, per se, about 'denial' but 'restriction' and control wherein desires are physically controlled for the mutual benefit of both partners or all those involved. Some think it should extend to both pain and pleasure to be complete; others disagree. Equally importantly, especially for newcomers, pornography misrepresents much of chastity – at the expense of the reality of passion and romance that many prefer and seek.

Part II
THE PRACTICE

Chastity, in various forms, can – as Larry Townsend noted many years ago and others have since confirmed – be achieved without using a device per se. However, for many, that's not the point. They need or want devices – and need information before they choose which to try and decide which then to use most.

This section seeks to 'identify the variables' that need to be taken into consideration when choosing devices – as well as then going on to offer some suggestions about how each of those variables should be assessed so that potential choices are as well informed as they can be. The most fundamental are listed here – although not in any particular order. Further factors that merit attention follow in Part III, covering 'Practicalities',

What quickly becomes clear when any man starts to think about locking is that finding and choosing a design that is practical for him demands careful consideration of the (potential) wearer's body shape and his way of life. Of course, the basic cost may appear the most immediate issue or greatest priority, but other factors are probably more important. (If any of us wants something enough, we're likely to find the motivation and patience to save, therefore choosing the most appropriate – or least inappropriate – design needs to be the first part of this process.)

Other factors include the duration of locking, allergies and piercings, for example. Thinking first and buying what appears to be a more expensive device may actually be cheaper in the long run and represent better value for money.

LIFE AND WORK

The two most immediate factors to consider are physical activity and working life. For those who are very physically active, some 'full' belts may be too restrictive around the waist for some forms of exercise, so a genital 'cage' may be more practical. While, for instance, others who intend being in their devices during working hours may find that security screening and office furniture are more major factors to consider.

Sedentary life

Many office chairs have been designed so that people sit leaning slightly forward, a posture that might not be sufficiently comfortable in some full belts for someone to work without being distracted inappropriately.

If you work in an office or have to sit for relatively long periods of time, positioning is all-important. Leaning even slightly forward, especially over a desk, sitting in even a well-designed an office chair, can be very uncomfortable while locked in a full belt with a metal front plate that doesn't have any 'give' or flexibility. Such plates can then dig into either the waist or chafe against the insides of the thighs while trying to sit with your legs together. Sitting more upright is not difficult, but may mean changing what has become a habit. The posture may also be better for your spine but, if a butt plug is in place, the pressure between the seat and the prostate may be greater. In many jurisdictions, employers *should* provide ergonomic office furniture – but explaining truthfully to an office manager why you require a particular design of chair may not always be socially or professionally acceptable or conventional. Take a trip to an office furniture store while locked and try out particular designs for comfort while sitting upright. The sales staff may even help put the chair in front of a desk with a keyboard and computer screen in, for you, their customary positions. Doing this, may help you identify a chair design that is best for you. Locked guys have been known to consult their doctors about discomfort in their lower backs while sitting in office seats – and getting letters to give to their managers recommending the provision of particular designs – without chastity ever being mentioned.

One Carrara wearer reported that getting accustomed to a slightly different position for driving his car took him a while too. Occupations where close physical contact, however unintentional, may also need to be taken into account, as brushing against someone may be enough to arouse suspicion. Such curiosity may, most of the time, be entirely innocuous; occasionally, it may be professionally awkward.

Greater activity

Those who are more active may find that full belt designs require greater compromise than cages. Many sporting activities can be difficult while wearing a metal waistband and a fairly substantial metal plate between one's legs, although they are no means impossible. Some gym exercises – such as sit-ups or crunches – and running can cause waistbands to chafe on the hips. Some guys fear the potential embarrassment of others involved in contact sports finding out about their predilections, which is understandable. Additionally, wearing a full belt could increase the risk of injury – both to the wearer and to others.

Those who want to use bicycles or motorcycles while locked in full belts may want to talk about the width and 'rise' of the front plate with the manufacturers when they are placing their orders. The ergonomic waistband designs developed by makers such as Walter Goethals and Neosteel have made life potentially less uncomfortable in such situations, but the front plate factors should be thought about before ordering rather than discovered the hard (and expensive) way afterwards.

Probably silicone devices are the least potentially dangerous to wear during sports; the material is flexible enough to absorb bumps without itself being damaged or damaging the wearer.

Those who are in active occupations – such as climbing up electricity supply poles or chasing around as law enforcement agents of some sort or another – may also consider that metal devices of any design are inappropriate. Again, silicone may be the least worst option.

Choosing clothing is important too – especially if you are potentially embarrassed or sensitive. However, if someone else is really to know that you are locked, they not only have to be looking quite carefully at the area between your legs, but they have to know enough about chastity to recognize the specific ridges that particular devices can create under everyday clothing. (This is considered in greater detail in Part III.)

Some men who are parents and live with children have expressed reservations about youngsters discovering devices when they are playing – and having to deal with childhood curiosity in a way that is honest and appropriate. Similarly, those whose work brings them into contact with children or 'vulnerable adults' may wish to consider devices that are potentially less obvious, either as far as unusual bulges are concerned or physical contact.

Clearly, in such circumstances, the understanding and co-operation of the keyholder or dominant is a great advantage. Will power and self-control may be required when locking is not considered suitable. Alternatively, where finances allow, some may choose to have more than one device – a polycarbonate or silicone design for during working or family hours and a metal one for other occasions. If they live together, arrangements can be made for the guy who is locked to change before or after work. If they don't then cell phone cameras can be used to provide evidence that devices are being changed without the guy who is locked abusing the opportunity.

DESIGN BASICS

Male chastity devices come in two basic forms. The first sort simply covers the penis, locked against a ring behind the genitals, usually now called a *cage*. The other type includes a penis tube, held behind a metal front plate, attached to a metal waistband and either metal thong between or straps at either side of the buttocks to hold the tube in place, called a *belt*. Together they have become chastity *devices*. A few designs also cover the balls – but most do not.

Answering 'frequently asked questions' (FAQs) on the Lockedmen website, Aarkey suggests that the two most important aspects of choosing devices are security (regarding the device staying in place) and 'wearability'. He recommends posting questions on various forums – but adds that responses can take weeks to appear. This section is an attempt to bring some of those questions and answers together. (A quick look at some online exchanges will confirm that such 'conversations' can include contributions that range from the practical, based on experience, to totally unrealistic fantasy. For beginners, differentiate them may not be as easy as it seems.)

The principal differences between cages and belts are the complexity and the cost. Cages can be bought relatively cheaply, especially online from manufacturers in China who disregard the intellectual property and development costs of designers elsewhere. Some cage makers only produce made-to-measure devices which, obviously, cost more. Belt designs that have not been crafted individually to conform to the body shape of the wearer may appear less expensive, but are unlikely to be sufficiently comfortable or robust to make the purchase really worthwhile.

Chastity enthusiasts posting questions and comments on the Fetlife website have raised questions such as the comfort of polycarbonate devices around, and behind, the scrotum, for example. One said he had had the opportunity to borrow and try a metal device – but added that the design was too expensive for him to get one made for himself. He also revealed that he had a Prince Albert piercing and asked about the strength of a one polycarbonate device with a 'seam' running lengthways along the shaft. This guy went on to say that he had a 'not-so-tiny grower' and that the tension on the balls and scrotum was unbearably uncomfortable whenever he had an erection.

One respondent helpfully suggested that, if the aim was to prevent sexual pleasure and ejaculations, but not erections, then a cap covering the glans might be a solution. However, the writer also posted a link to one of the more expensive manufacturers of custom-made devices.

The 2014 online research for the Lockedmen website revealed that more than 70 per cent – or nearly 650 – of those responding to the questions said they had been locked in 'genuine' (polycarbonate) CB series devices while 23 per cent had experienced the silicone Bon 4 or Birdlocked designs and 16 per cent had been in Mature Metal products. Another 12 per cent had been locked in US-made metal cages and about the same number had been in Holy Trainer devices. Nearly 10 per cent had been locked in Chinese-made plastic devices while 10 per cent had been in metal designs from Steelworxx in Germany, 6.6 per cent (or 60 guys) had been in either Carrara or Goethals belts from Belgium and a similar number had been in other full belts; 28 respondents (3 per cent) had been in Neosteel products. The 'other' full belt designs were identified as Latowski products by 5.4 per cent – or seven – of the respondents.

General consensus attitudes towards which general design or which particular brand or model may be best for any particular individual are almost impossible to glean from the thousands of reviews that are now available on a myriad of websites. The main reason for this is that those contributing their opinions either fail to provide sufficient information about themselves, their body shapes, ways of life or their chastity requirements that the assessments are not as helpful to others as they could be. If such details are available, insufficient work has – yet – been done scientifically or academically to correlate these 'lifestyle' factors with each model. Consequently, the assessments here may appear equally general. However, they should become more valuable in making individual decisions when all the other factors – listed in both this section and the next – are taken into consideration.

Devices that enclose the entire genitals, especially if they are solid with only a relatively small hole at the bottom as a 'piss drain' are generally impractical for more than a few hours as they are exceedingly difficult to keep dry and clean. One type also includes a strip of Velcro which could become unpleasantly smelly and moist quite quickly.

Cages

For several years, the polycarbonate devices such as the CB2000 series were the only alternatives to heavy metal belts such as those produced by Tollyboy and Access Denied. Even then, they were not cheap – and consequently remained beyond the means of many.

The devices were, however, well engineered, with a finish that indicated that the designer and manufacturers knew what they were doing. With a choice of sizes – from the relatively small CB2000 to the more generous Curve – they also recognized the great anatomical variations with other versions too. These devices, produced by AL Enterprises Inc in the United States, each came with five 'base' cockrings so that they fitted most men.

Aarkey noted that the CB2000 was wider and shorter but easier to clean while the CB3000 and CB6000 are each a more 'natural' shape and medium-sized while the Curve's profile can make it more visible under some clothing.

A manufacturer called Novamedia introduced the silicone 'Birdlocked' designs in 2008 and, together with the CB series (or the many counterfeit facsimiles made in, and sold from, China); they appear to have become the most recognized, if not the most popular, non-metal basic designs. The one-piece design includes a triangular base or anchor ring said to be more comfortable around the scrotum. The tube of the Swiss-made silicone Dickcage designs extends from a broad band around the cock and balls while the Birdlocked is not quite so all-encasing. The Birdlocked 'Pico' design includes 17 small silicone 'tips' to deter erections. One review says these are 'flexible, but prolonged use causes extreme sensation'. The Holy Trainer silicone device has been described as 'half angel, half demon'. Colors can vary too. Some devices are only available in a light gray, while others have been produced in black, different shades of blue, yellow, pink and a camouflage design.

All cages include a tube for the penis which sits, pointing downwards over the balls. The angle varies between the designs, but longer devices, such as the Curve, wrap over the sac. Some have bars while others have holes – which allow both some airflow for ventilation and water flow for cleaning. Many devices offer tubes in a selection of diameters. If the tube is too wide, then getting out can be easy, too narrow and the flesh of the shaft will push into the holes, possibly uncomfortably and making cleaning difficult.

The Exobelt – which is really a cage – is reported to be very comfortable and one website claims that it is possible for the wearer to urinate while standing. Others have suggested that a disadvantage is its profile – which may be more prominent under clothing. Some guys with balls have said they found the design impractical, but opinions clearly vary.

Cages with too few openings and which fit closely against the penis are, logically, more difficult to keep clean, so design – rather than material per se – may be a factor influencing the purchase decision which requires greater attention.

Some designs are more imaginative. The Lancelot, for example, looks as if it is made from chain mail – but is in fact steel mesh. The look is quite dramatic and the shape is said to be flexible enough to adapt to the position and contours of the wearer although cleanliness may be more difficult than for those in simpler devices.

The Lori's tube design has been available for longer than many others and includes extra security that uses a steel screw through a piercing such as a Prince Albert. The variety of metal cages available in 2015 is extensive. They assortment extends from the US-made Mature Metal range – which includes designs with bars or broader metal bands – to some similar styles from Gerecke Keuschheitsgürtel.

Probably the most exclusive, most glorious and most desired devices are those custom-made by Steelwerks Extreme in Montreal, Canada. They produce custom-made designs in either steel or titanium and have found a niche market at what can best be described as the haute-couture end of the chastity scale. The workmanship is superb and the imagination behind some of the designs is most beautifully devious.

Many metal cages are available with extras – such as urethral plugs and tubes or attachments that run between the legs to metal balls for prostate and anal stimulation. Custom-made devices may be any length, so individual requirements, such as that for greater constraint for example, may be possible.

Belts

Similarly, belt designs have some characteristics in common. Most enclose the penis in a metal tube which then points downwards. The Tollyboy and Neosteel patterns have front plates which push the balls outward to the sides with the waistbands of each locking above these plates. The Goethals designs, in contrast, have a waistband that goes into each side of an adjustable locking plate. The Carrara design from Goethals additionally has a covering for the balls while the Latowski also completely encases the genitals. The rear fixing can either be with a single metal or chain thong, often covered in rubber, set between the cheeks or jockstrap-like chains to each side.

The Tollyboy has, for example, been described – in historic terms – as 'traditionally Florentine', while the metal of the LockedinSteel alternative is silicone-covered with a one-piece locking mechanism; escape is said to be impossible. Another design, in contrast, includes a covering for the entire male genitals that in some ways resembles a 'protector' used by sportsmen while a third has an extremely narrow plate in front of the tube for the cock.

The Latowski is more like metal underwear, the 'brief' shaping covering the entire pubic area with a back that more substantial than simply a thong between the buttocks. Simpler belt designs include the German-made CS-100 and the My-Steel and NeoSteel, also from Germany. Most simple of all are probably penis tubes attached with single steel links to waistbands by Fancy Steel of Australia.

Sheaths

Some *sheaths* are also now available. Some cover the glans of the penis while (some of) the shaft may still available for stimulation, but penetration is probably impractical. Others surround the shaft but leave the glans uncovered. Both designs can, of course, be exploited by a Dom.

Again, the choice seems to be between polycarbonate and metal.

A polycarbonate model – the PA-5000 from AL Enterprises – is anchored in place using a lock through a Prince Albert piercing. This does allow (some of) the glans to be uncovered so the device could probably be manipulated backwards and forwards to emulate masturbation, so preventing (comfortable or pleasurable) penetration but not preclude orgasm or ejaculation.

Metal alternatives, such as the Kali's Teeth Bracelet along the shaft, may appear quite extreme – but (despite some reservations) they can apparently be worn for quite long periods of time, although, as one man said, they take 'some getting used to'. Sharper teeth can cause more damage, more easily and more quickly, and can be more painful should the penis swell at all while blunt teeth can be more bearable. Some dominants have been known to use such devices on their submissives without any direct restrictions regarding the stimulation of the cock or limitations on ejaculation or orgasm. Their approach is that if a submissive is prepared to ensure the discomfort during the process and the soreness afterwards, then that is their decision. One guy I know has reported being allowed to masturbate while in a Kali's Teeth device – and occasionally even being ordered to do so – but he knows that doing so will probably damage the skin to the extent of drawing blood. Healing usually, he said, takes several days and the generous use of medicated unguents to minimize any infection risks. Some speculate that the pain of spikes can create the equivalent in the autonomic nervous system of 'muscle memory' so that the penis learns not to attempt to get hard. Other dominants work from the hypothesis that the fear of the discomfort may be sufficient to deter arousal.

Alternatively, the Buddy-Lock is reported to be very solid, with a cage material that resists acids, sweat and salt water while the steel retaining 'arc' does not include any nickel.

MATERIALS

Attitudes about the relative pros and cons of the materials used in chastity cage designs vary radically, even passionately. I have encountered one guy posting on websites who is determinedly against 'plastic' – personally arguing that it is less hygienic than metal. I have to say that I disagree with this bland generalization. I would argue that the 'inert' properties of AL Enterprises CB range are such that they are no more likely to cause problems because of perspiration, for example, than many metal designs.

Cages with too few openings and which fit closely against the penis are, logically, more difficult to keep clean, so design – rather than material per se – is the factor which requires greater attention.

The 'softer', more flexible and pliable silicone ranges are probably more likely to increase sweating, because they do not allow the skin to breathe as easily as harder materials. These shouldn't, for example, be impractical for guys who are jumping into swimming pools several times a day – but for those wearing business suits, in well-heated offices, who are not moving around much during the working day, then personal hygiene may be more of a concern.

Opinions of the three principal materials used for devices – polycarbonate, silicone and metal – vary, although many of those offering their views online seemed to have tried two of these but not always all three.

One guy who had tried two said he preferred a metal device to a polycarbonate one – as keeping clean in that was difficult without removing the device and rubbing make his glans sore, which took a long time to heal. 'I have had my metal one on for 87 days ... with no problems other than some discomfort once in a while, which is to be expected.'

Another said metal was easier to keep clean while another said that while stainless steel was the 'way to go' for long-term locking, polycarbonate devices such as the CB series were hard to beat as a first device, especially with so many variations to help someone find the 'right' individual fit. 'Then,' he added, 'once you are good with both the idea and the fit, go metal. I have a (Mature Metal) Jailbird on for 24 hours a day for more than two years with just a few releases a year, but I could never have got the sizing right unless I had had the CB6000s first.'

This approach was supported – with the advice: 'Don't rush in. Enjoy the journey. Go slowly.' Another said that trying a less expensive polycarbonate device would let someone discover whether they were 'into this kink or not' (but without appearing to acknowledge that the wearer may have abdicated any choice in the matter).

Another was a very keen advocate of metal: 'No splitting,' he said, 'no need to remove for cleaning, no stinking, a long life, the only issue is security gates' before adding: 'Nowadays, I am blunt enough to tell the security personnel that I am chaste and asking them if they'd like to see (the device). Not one has asked to unzip and show.'

'The silicone models I have tried,' said another guy, 'have not been comfortable as they grip and pull on the skin and can be quite bulky. I love metal, but all devices – no matter how open they are – require cleaning.' He added that, for him, the 'thing' with metal is the weight, saying: 'The feel of heavy metal wrapped around your gear is great'. He also reported that he used both plastic and metal devices for 'variety and practicality', using plastic when he was travelling and metal at home. 'When I was sure of the fit with the plastic, I ordered exactly the same fit in metal, but a different model,' he added.

Although most metal devices are made from surgical quality stainless steel, allergic reactions may nevertheless occasionally occur. As with piercings, titanium may be better – but potentially far more expensive. Steelwerks Extreme in Montreal indicate that titanium is about 40 per cent lighter in weight than steel but costs about 50 per cent more.

Posts regularly appear on chastity websites warning about the dangers of some inexpensive devices – as many purporting to be made of steel are cheap chrome-plated zinc. 'They don't last,' one guy said, 'and can pinch unexpectedly in places no guy wants to be pinched.' Online retailers often only have knock-offs for sale too. 'Many,' the guy added, 'only last for the first couple of uses, then the seams split and when they pinch, they do not let go.' Some cheaper cages, genuinely made from steel, are available – but the quality varies. 'I have,' he added, 'seen steel knock-offs fail'. The welding is weak and counterfeiters will not honor any warranties either, he said.

SECURITY

The question of security is a particularly vexed one that confronts most guys who are being locked. Some guys use 'extras' – such as the 'points of intrigue' available for the polycarbonate CB range. These sharp studs dig into the flesh of the penis, increasing the difficulty of pulling out. Sharp points can damage the skin, more seriously than chafing, increasing infection risks as well as potentially being more painful for longer than may originally have been intended. Smoothing the points with emery paper can reduce the potential for skin damage while not detracting too much from their purpose. Some men report that the sensation from these is enough to prevent any attempt at erection while others have said that, if they are active, they can very quickly cause sores that require the removal of the device for long enough to allow healing.

Even then, security is not guaranteed. The type of penis being locked also needs to be taken into account. The male form seems to best be characterized in two extremes – the 'show-er' or the 'grower'. The show-er is a guy who always shows what he has got, even when flaccid. The penis may rise when erect, but its size remains relatively constant. The grower, in contrast, may be very small when flaccid but increase substantially in size when excited. Of course, no two men are likely to meet each stereotype completely; everyone varies within the two parameters. Men who are 'growers' have each reported that the penis can shrink so much that they can pull it back out of the device. However, many also report that getting the cock back into a device that is locked in place may be far more difficult, if not impossible, so providing the keyholder with evidence of the escape. Others suggest that a man's balls feel different, perhaps fuller, when release has been denied for a period of time, a characteristic a keyholder may learn to notice.

Aarkey has also noted that – for 'growers' rather than 'show-ers' – the 'keepsake' addition for CB devices that goes around the base of the penis can be effective, but that some users have reported that it can restrict the flow of blood and/or urine. As with so much of many devices, personal adjustments may well be necessary.

Additionally, if a locked guy is going to make a commitment to a keyholder, then escaping – possibly for a relatively short period of time and unsatisfactory masturbation – undermines both the physical predicament and the emotional rapport between those involved. Why, as one guy asked, would I want to spoil the achievement of being locked for several weeks with a quick wank in a toilet? If you want to be locked up, said another, you want to be locked up; why go to the trouble of trying to escape? 'Submission,' he added, 'is far more powerful than a device, even if you use a device along with submission.'

However, if it is not already apparent, the most effective security approach of all, it seems, is using piercings – such as a Prince Albert – each with its own separate lock or shackle to prevent the penis being pulled out of any device.

Nevertheless, it is important not to forget that the question of security can only be answered in the context of what is being prevented, or what the wearer and keyholder want to prevent. The nature of the chastity must be defined first: is the control to prevent penetration? To prevent contact with the cock? To prevent ejaculation? To prevent orgasms entirely? Honesty is paramount – as some guys can achieve ejaculatory orgasms without any contact with their cocks whatsoever. Others can 'wank their balls' to achieve 'ball-gasms' while others can achieve orgasm and ejaculate as a result of anal stimulation. Some guys say that, when they are deprived of the sensations created by the stimulation of the cock, their anuses take on a greater sensitivity and they become far more aware of the area and its musculature. Even those who have previously not achieved much pleasure from anal stimulation report that this changes significantly when their cocks are locked away. Other locked guys have reported being able to achieve orgasm and ejaculation while locked by using vibrators – either pressed against the base of the cock above the balls or at the point where the sac meets the perineum between the legs.

SIZING AND COMFORT

Comfort may not be entirely the best word to use in this context as some keyholders and dominants do argue that a degree of discomfort and the perpetual awareness of their predicament are important for some who are locked. Setting aside this nuance, the uncertainty remains in finding a design that is both affordable and will not be so uncomfortable that it becomes a ceaseless distraction from aspects of everyday living – such as work.

A crucial factor identified in many website postings seems to be the size – in many designs – of the 'base' ring, the one situated behind the cock and balls. Those rings with are 'segmented' seem more likely to chafe, even where any hinges or joins have protective coverings. The second key factor is size. The ring needs to be tight enough to prevent one or both of the balls escaping while simultaneously not being so tight that the blood flow to the balls, sac and penis is badly affected. If this happens, the balls can become swollen and even painful. Men with tight ball sacs may appreciate more discomfort, with the sac trying to shrink back against a base ring, than those with low hangers. Ball sac stretching can be achieved – but a key factor for many is temperature. Nature has designed the scrotum to be elastic, allowing the testes to be kept at the optimum temperature for sperm production. So, in warmer circumstances, the sac will loosen, allowing the balls to move away a little from the heat of the torso. In the cold, the opposite will happen. So, as well as individual anatomy, climatological circumstances probably need to be considered too. Those who live and work in warmer climes are potentially less likely to experience the soreness resulting from sacs trying to retreat, while perhaps experiencing more chafing because they perspire more.

Most, but not all, cage designs rely on the base ring as the anchoring point. Some full belts may have rings of some sort that encircle the genitals. Some manufacturers also produce base rings that are anatomically shaped so that they fit more comfortably against the contours of the pelvis while others are oval rather than circular. While the designers have intended that the joints of segmented rings should remain at 'the back' behind the scrotum and against the perineum, they can, and do, move around very easily – and inconveniently. Trying to adjust devices so that they are correctly positioned may not be easy and may not be achievable without attracting unwanted attention. Some manufacturers – such as AL Enterprises – supply base rings of several sizes with their CB designs while the silicone Pico range has base rings that are adjustable. Men who are 'show-ers' are probably likely to find it easier to find (cage) devices that fit them more comfortably for more of the time. They may find that pressure increases, along with discomfort, as the angle of the penis tries to change while becoming erect, but they are less likely to experience the greater distress that can be caused when a growing cock pushes against a cage, pulling the back ring along the shaft and also possibly squeezing the balls.

Choosing the right size of ready-made base rings may not be easy, especially for men who regard themselves as having large penises and small balls or small penises and large balls. Sometimes getting the balls through base rings that are then quite comfortable and practical can be difficult. While this may not be unduly problematic for someone who is only occasionally unlocked – to go through security scanners for example – for others, the process can become easier with practice. Knowing the shape and size of each testicle may help. Most are oblate spheroids and more oval than a hen's egg while, for many guys, the left is often slightly bigger than the right. The cock, when flaccid, can usually be squashed more – and less painfully than the balls – so getting the balls through the ring first may be easiest. Using a lubricant can help, but probably needs wiping away soon as possible so that the balls do not, immediately and unintentionally, escape again.

Choosing the correct anchor ring is not straightforward either. The metal or other material used may be elliptical rather than round, a shape that – for some – may cause extra rubbing and chafing. Some rings are hinged – and the hinges may also chafe behind the scrotum. An 'anatomical' ring designed by Steelworxx in Germany does not lie flat; it is bent slightly to emulate the contours of the pubis.

Sizing is a matter of personal preference too. Some guys like the constraint to be great while others find than having more room is less potentially uncomfortable for longer locking periods. For some, a very small cage that further diminishes the size of the cock adds to feelings of emasculation or the small penis/big penis aspect of dominance versus submission. 'Growers' have reported that cage designs that allow some room for expansion can be too loose when they are totally flaccid.

Similarly, those men whose penises are thicker have said that finding devices that fit them has been difficult. Some recommend metal rather than polycarbonate devices. One online question elicited the suggestion that a silicone device may be larger while a second respondent suggested the Curve, implying extra width would be achieved at the compromise of extra length too.

One guy said he really liked his CS-100 device but found that the underside of his cock became very sore after a few days. 'When I get hard,' he said, 'it presses against the entrance ring of the tube and the pressure eventually abrades my skin.' This is, he suggested, a fairly common problem with the design. He wondered if cushioning this with a ring of soft, perhaps rubber-like, material around his cock would solve the problem. He said this would have to be OK for permanent wear, waterproof and reasonably hygienic – as he was unlocked for cleaning about once a week – and soft, flexible and reasonably thin.

One respondent suggested dropping some baby oil gel on the edge of the tube as this 'works wonders' while advising against rubber products as they can stick to the skin and exacerbate such problems. 'Also,' this writer added, 'after some time, your skin may become tougher.'

Some guys have reported that silicone does not 'breathe' so they find themselves perspiring more – and, when the perspiration evaporates, they become dry in a way that can be uncomfortable. Dripping baby oil or something similar down inside the cage tube can be one way to prevent this.

Erections – especially at night – can exacerbate the way a device rubs. Similarly, if a device can move about, either under clothing or during sleep, chafing can very easily and relatively quickly occur. Some guys deal with this by using balms of some sort as a preventative approach before bed while others use them for relief afterwards. Others choose a style of underwear that reduces the motion – even as nightwear.

Once more, the anecdotal consensus seems to be that these uncomfortable sensations are less likely to be experienced when the cock has developed what could be described as the penile equivalent of 'muscle memory'. The body will learn that erections are potentially painful – and, over time, they may become less frequent or less intense. (The potency – as the section on unlocking in Part III of this book on Practicalities explains – is however likely to return too.) Being aware that this may well happen and being ready for such discomfort could enable a locked guy to prepare himself mentally to get through this phase of longer-term locking without 'freaking out' and demanding irrational release.

Polycarbonate spacing bars supplied with the CB series of devices, for example, can be cut and trimmed with a sharp knife or scalpel blade – available from craft or hobby stores. This can only be done once, so do not be impatient; make sure that different variations are tried for long enough and during a range of fairly frequent activities to make sure that the fit is the best possible. Emery board should be used to make sure the edges are as smooth as possible after cutting.

Polycarbonate devices – such as the CB range produced by AL Enterprises in the United States – come with (white plastic) bars to hold the device in place. Getting these to be the right length is a process that should not be hurried. Each comes with several spacer rings and finding the most comfortable and practical combination can take time, often at least a week of everyday wear, perhaps even longer. For some designs, the rods will poke through the 'anchor' ring again rub against the pubic area. That can be made less uncomfortable by winding a cotton handkerchief around the cock and balls behind the 'anchor' ring. Changing the handkerchief at least every day is recommended – especially in temperatures that trigger perspiration – while the wearer gets used to pissing while locked. The bars can then be cut when the most comfortable combination has been found and tested for long enough.

Wrapping 'back ring' hinges in Band-Aid or similar medical adhesive tape may reduce the chafing, but will need to be replaced frequently, either because of hygiene or because it is difficult to dry after showering or swimming. Some manufacturers provide plastic covers for the hinges, but these too need removing regularly for cleaning.

Probably the best way of alleviating the discomfort of chafing quickly is with zinc and caster oil cream, sold in drug stores as a remedy for diaper rash and so usually found on the baby products aisle. The consistency is quite thick but it also washes out of clothing quite easily, unlike greasier alternatives. That said, good, old-fashioned Vaseline has its place too, especially because the small containers sold as 'lip therapy' are such a convenient size. (They are also easy to refill from bigger, cheaper containers.)

Some devices may include screws through the anchor ring that can be tightened to dig into the flesh of the genitals. Similarly, keeping these in place for long periods of activity can result in the skin being broken and infection risks increasing. They are, consequently, probably more practical for times when the wearer is relatively motionless.

Circumcision

The consensus from some chastity websites seems to be that men who are not circumcised can find it more difficult than cut guys to find devices they like and then, after being locked, with personal hygiene.

Obviously, pulling the foreskin back for washing or pinching it closed to rinse around the glans with fresh urine is impossible for a guy who is locked. Then, those with longer foreskins have reported that they can find this gets caught in the small holes at the ends of some devices. One guy said his foreskin covers the head of his penis in a cage – potentially becoming very messy quite quickly. Trying to keep the foreskin pulled back can become very uncomfortable quite quickly as – even in a cage – the glans is quite sensitive and doing so can be impractical, even using medical adhesive tape.

Some manufacturers – who themselves have experience of being locked – will discuss the practicalities of foreskins for those who are ordering custom-made devices. And, for example, Mature Metal say on their website they had found that 'reversing the bars on the front of the cage pushes the clothing away from the end and prevents pinching'.

PIERCINGS

The Prince Albert (PA) – involving a hole on the underside of the glans – is probably the most popular, strongest and most practical body piercing for many men. The hole itself is relatively small in terms of the thickness of the flesh through which it goes. The installation procedure is very fast and healing does not take long. Getting a PA is quick and easy too. Many professional piercers will install PAs relatively cheaply. The pain may be intense but momentary, lasting no more than two or three seconds probably. Some professional piercers may have the appropriate medical licenses that allow them to use injectable anaesthetics. (That said, the fear of a very small diameter hypodermic needle used for an anaesthetic is far greater for many than the – take a deep breath – actual sensation when it goes in.) Others wanting to numb the nearby nerve endings use topical creams containing mild anaesthetics, such as those intended to relieve the discomfort of haemorrhoids or, in some jurisdictions, the liquid oral anaesthetics that are available in pharmacies for relieving toothache.

The rings – or partial rings – that can go through the holes may be fairly small at first, say no more than 3 or 4 millimeters, but they can then be stretched quite quickly. Such rings are 'easier to manage' for men who are circumcised but many guys with foreskin enjoy having PAs too.

Getting one at a time of the year when the climate allows a guy to stroll around naked or in baggy shorts so that lots of air gets to the area can accelerate healing as can drinking a lot, so pissing frequently rinses the area. (Remember though that aiming at a standard diameter toilet bowl immediately becomes twice as difficult because a guy is trying to control two holes rather than one – and that sitting will probably be more sensible as well as being a lot less messy.)

Having a small padlock through a PA piercing alone may be enough to prevent most men from indulging in penetrative sex – as the device could so significant physical damage to a vagina or anus. Having a padlock in your mouth is also unlikely to enhance fellatio; as well as potential hygiene concerns regarding the cleanliness of the lock, teeth aren't intended to cope with being bashed by such pieces of metal. Additionally, a padlock alone is clearly insufficient to prevent masturbation – but, depending on the requirements of a relationship – may provide enough control to satisfy both a lockee and a keyholder. Remember too that a small padlock, like a large single item of genital jewellery may be sufficient to trigger the security scanners used at airports and some government or other public buildings.

Locks with hasps small enough to go through PAs should be inspected and checked carefully before being used. The metal may be an alloy that contains impurities that cause allergic reactions. Some guys cope perfectly well with surgical quality stainless steel while others prefer the hypoallergenic qualities of titanium. The internal mechanisms of some locks – even famous international proprietary brands – may not be waterproof and can rush and seize very quickly, even within hours. Most of the now well-known manufacturers of custom-made cages also produce locks that can be used with PAs – and other piercings.

A PA can also be used as an anchoring point for a 'Prince's Wand' or urethral probe – adding, if necessary, a further relatively short-term dimension to any control or power transfer that accompanies being locked. PAs can also be attached to *guiche* piercings; rings that are inserted a few millimeters into the flesh of the perineum between the legs. The metal usually goes through at least a centimeter or nearly half an inch of flesh – so healing can be a slow process.

However, once both have 'settled', PA and guiche piercings can be linked together, pulling the penis down over the ball sac. Any arousal will create tension on both piercings, but the flesh of the shaft is still uncovered and available for stimulation. This may be uncomfortable and penetration may be impossible but stimulation, even to orgasm or ejaculation, remains possible.

Many guys recommending finding practitioners who are licensed to use anaesthetics for getting piercings such as guiches because the holes are far longer than those of PAs. While a piercing needle is going through the flesh, the body's autonomic nervous system may 'trip in', however much the piercee exercises self control. If this happens and the body moves unintentionally, however little, the point of the needle may 'nick' an otherwise entirely smooth channel. While these flaws may appear miniscule, they represent potential weak points that are more susceptible to infection or soreness which may get in the way of future use and play.

Healing times vary greatly – but the consensus of advice from guys online is that a piercing should not be used as an anchor for a chastity device until it really has healed fully and, with PAs, the cock gets accustomed to the size and weight of the metal ring.

Manufacturers such as Steelworxx in Germany and Steelwerks Extreme in Montreal, Canada, produce lockable shackles or other designs specifically intended for use with piercings. However, for those men with more genital piercings, finding compatible devices could be difficult. For example, a 'ladder' of bars along the cock could be either disproportionately uncomfortable or be more difficult to keep clean in a cage, while scrotal piercings of any sort may not sit easily inside a Carrara design or if the balls are pushed out sideways by a Neosteel front plate while piercing cleanliness may be a little more difficult within the confinements of a Latowski, for instance.

Introducing ritual

Getting a piercing, especially an intimate one, can be a very intimate, shared experience. Many professional piercers appreciate this and will, with notice, be willing to make arrangements so that a partner (and perhaps even other witnesses) can be present. As well as the physical techniques, they appreciate that they could enhance the occasion by the way they behave and interact with those involved. Those who carry out genital piercings are also unlikely to be embarrassed when they are introduced to someone who is locked in chastity.

Even if a locked man is to travel to a piercer with a cage or other device in place, full cleaning as near to the time of the journey is recommended. Similarly, allowing time for full healing before re-locking is generally advisable.

COST

Cost is clearly an issue for many guys – and their partners or keyholders. Custom-made devices that are probably the most secure are not cheap. Research carried out by the chastitytrophy.com website in 2015 indicated that the prices of legitimate – rather than counterfeit – devices can range from about 100 euros (or about US $115 at spring 2015 exchange rates) – to several thousand.

The site collated information to try to find the most popular devices. They listed the prices, in euros, in May 2015 but no indication was given about whether the sums included sales taxes or shipping. The Tollyboy website (in April 2015) was showing that it had not been updated since 2010 or 2011.

MEASURING

Measuring may not be easy. Reading a tape measure clearly in some postures can be intricate – and some dimensions needed for custom-made full belts may be nearly impossible to calculate by a man on his own. Establishing the size of the 'anchor' cock (and ball) ring is relatively straightforward, if a little time consuming. Buying a range of simple metal cockrings of different sizes and wearing each for a few days, throughout every activity, is one way of finding out which is sufficiently snug to be practical to remain in place without causing discomfort. Getting used to wearing a (metal) cockring before being locked into chastity can also help the body become accustomed to the change. In the cold, the sac shrinks to hold the balls more closely against the warmth of the body; wearing a cockring stops this happening and may, at first, be quite noticeable.

More difficult to get right is the distance between the metal or plastic ring that encircles both the cock and balls and one that just goes around the cock. That space needs to be adequate to prevent undue pressure on the scrotum and balls while simultaneously being too small to allow the balls to squeeze back through the 'anchor' ring. Ironically, while even very conscientious testing may indicate that a ring is the correct size, bending down once can undermine such research unintentionally within seconds. Finding that one ball has 'popped back' though the anchor ring may be disconcerting *and* uncomfortable. Getting the ball back through the ring may be impossible so, if the guy in chastity and the keyholder are not likely to see each other within a few hours, strategies need to be found so the wearer can unlock, replace the ball and re-lock as quickly as possible.

As far as anyone thinking about a full belt is concerned, measuring is not easy, whether someone is trying or their own or being helped by someone else who also does not necessarily appreciate the nuances of the operation as much as a skilled and experienced manufacturer. Some have encountered difficulties when devices have been made to the specifications that were provided but, when turned from a flexible tape measure to the rigidity of metal, the fit still leaves much to be desired. Customer and after-sales service does vary, but the consensus seems to be that most major manufacturers respect potential buyers enough to be ready to help them – either on the phone, in person or through e-mail or other electronic communication. Anyone who is in any doubt about measuring for a particular device should have no hesitation in asking for advice and assistance; a few minutes spent helping someone get an order right before work starts is probably time far better spent for a maker than having to deal with later alterations for someone who could, otherwise, be very disappointed.

Going 3-D

The advent of '3D printers' – computer-controlled machines that extrude plastic – has started adding yet another dimension to chastity devices. Aficionados can create, and then test, their own devices in a way that is relatively affordable.

Some skilled designers have not only been so amazingly imaginative and technically skilled that they have created some devices, they have – through discussions with users and keyholders using the chat room and messaging facilities on websites such as LockedMen – responded to the ideas and suggestions of users.

The technology behind individual plastic extrusion means that 'made-to-measure' devices can now be produced in ways that had, until relatively recently, only been practical using metal.

Fortunately, those interested in chastity include men with skills as designers and engineers whose interests also include materials science. One pioneer in Europe has collaborated closely with users by exchanging messages using the online forums section of the Lockedmen website. Indeed, Pedro69 has, among this small community, won great acclaim for his efforts. In mid-2015, his designs could be found on two websites: www.shapeways.com/shops/pedro69 and www.sculpteo.com/en/s/pedroitaly

The website discussions have covered aspects of the designs such as urination, soreness and sizing. Checking the latest additions to the discussion may be worthwhile before placing an order.

Part III
AND PRACTICALITIES

The topics in this section have all been raised by guys interested in chastity. They are listed alphabetically rather than in order of importance or significance.

ANAL CONTROL

For some guys, the idea of anal chastity – the prevention of that sort of penetration – appeals too. This may, for example, relate to penetration by a person, either with fingers, a penis or a strap-on dildo, but not to penetration with a plug kept in place for a length of time. Some full belt devices are designed so that butt plugs can be attached and locked into place; Geothals' designs have screw fittings that are inaccessible without unlocking, for example.

The 'Healthy Bear' – a gay general practitioner (or primary care physician) living and working in Melbourne, Australia, wrote on his website that ... 'very little research has been done on the topic' (of using butt plugs), which considering the nature of the activity and general public (if not private) attitudes is not really surprising. He added that the 'majority of the information is anecdotal and based on medical common sense'.

Having a plug *locked* in place is potentially risky not least because immediate removal is advised if a wearer reports or experiences unusual discomfort or bleeding. If a plug is locked in, that may not be possible as quickly as some medics would recommend. The Healthy Bear explained that, more than two or three inches inside, skin-like nerves disappear, so sensations may be different. Users can take a while to learn how to identify what happens to this particular part of their bodies before going on to develop the awareness necessary to monitor themselves effectively. Cramps, irritation and bloating sensations may indicate damage, he added. He also said that the edges of some plug designs 'can squeeze the delicate lining of the anus between the sphincter and the toy, decreasing the local blood flow and, if prolonged, can cause damage or ulceration.' For this reason, he advises against wearing butt plugs for more than two to three hours at a time, even when comfortable.

Some advocates and enthusiasts clearly wear plugs for far longer than this. Obviously, taking this point into consideration suggests that, for longer use, more elliptical designs – rather than those with sharper ridges – would be less likely to put disproportionate pressure on any of the internal membranes. Those who do prefer longer locking anecdotally suggest that the body needs to become accustomed to such 'invasion' gradually – perhaps starting with being plugged for an hour each day for a few days before extending this to two hours, then three and gradually more. Some also suggest that the size of the plug is increased incrementally over time too.

The adage that what goes in must come out should not be forgotten either. Foods that are processed and purified are generally considered more likely to cause constipation, because they contain insufficient roughage. Internal impacting is not good. Limiting the intake of solids may seem like a good idea, especially if chastity and plugging are being combined with a weight loss program. However, human metabolism does require a balanced intake, with roughage being particularly important for bowel health, so choosing a predominantly liquid diet – even of wholesome vegetable broths and soups for example rather than alcohol – for more than a day or two cannot really be advised.

The anus, rectum and lower intestine should be thoroughly clean before a plug is inserted – and retained – for a significant period of time; in other words, probably any longer than an hour or two. However, over-enthusiastic use of douches on shower attachments can very easily also wash away beneficial mucus on the internal membranes. Some aficionados of anal activity recommend using – and holding – a first enema of salt water; a process that they suggest helps retain the mucus. For those on low sodium diets because of high blood pressure, although no empirical research appeared (by mid-2014) to have been published, the potassium salt sold as a culinary alternative may be worth considering in this context.

The rectum is intended as a storage silo for shit, so filling the space with a large plug will keep the excrement backed up, potentially blocking the lower intestine. Simply challenging anatomical evolution with plugging for too long does not, inherently, seem very wise. Therefore, common sense would suggest that a regime of long periods of plugging should allow periods perhaps two or three times a day, rather than just once, when the bowels can be evacuated as fully as possible, perhaps assisted by douching or using (glycerine) suppositories. It is worth repeating that the Healthy Bear also advised that if pain or bleeding lasts for more than a few minutes after a plug is removed, then medical help should be sought immediately.

Cleaning butt toys thoroughly is important. Using lots of water is the best way to dilute any infectious agent, so that is the best start. The Healthy Bear recommends that, after rinsing with as hot water as possible, use an antibacterial soap others then add that a soft cloth can help. Scrubbing brushes or anything that could scratch the toy should be avoided, to avoid damage and any nicks. Leaving toys to dry in the air is probably best and then storing each – in individual plastic bags – will prevent one damaging another. Some guys recommend putting them through the dishwasher, but check the material, temperature and whether any detergent is needed. The abrasiveness of the salt required by some dishwasher designs or incorporated in cleaning 'tablets' may not be entirely good for such toys. Checking with the retailer or the manufacturer for the best 'care' advice is probably very sensible.

As well as anal control through insertion, penetration may also be prevented in a way that some may consider to be more extreme. This continues the concept of chastity that has, during some periods in the past, been directed towards preventing penetration by the recipient or passive partner. Historical documents, either written accounts or illustrations, and some surviving medieval devices themselves confirm that the intention was to prevent vaginal penetration. In many cultures and for many generations, anal penetration has been tacitly acceptable between men and women as a form of sexual release (for the guy) without any risk of conception. So, while chastity – in the 21st century – seems to be more focused on controlling the penis, and potential orgasms, of the male as an 'active' partner, scope nevertheless remains for controlling a man's anus.

But why? Simply transferring the decision about when a man may defecate can be part of a power-transfer relationship or interaction. Making a (submissive) guy wait can be a very intimate means of exercising control. The risks of mess are relatively few, especially if, for example, a man is instructed to wait in a bathroom, aware of the toilet facilities but denied their use. Alternatively, such control can be linked, for the aficionados, to diaper 'play' and use.

Depending on someone's diet, the person exercising control should be sensible enough to keep the submissive very aware of his predicament, but only for long enough to avoid the possibility of 'impacting' what's inside and avoiding potential constipation. Also, such control can be associated with dynamics such as the loss of privacy and internal cleanliness, using douching or enemas.

Stimulating the prostate, as has been discussed elsewhere, can be a beautifully frustrating way of gently arousing a man whose penis is unavailable for direct stimulation. As well as relatively conventional butt plugs of various shapes and sizes, some have also become available which can be locked in place. While these should be used very carefully, especially if the person who is impaled is expected to move around and not inserted until after 'evacuation' and internal cleansing, they can remain in place for several hours. Unlike some plug designs, where the 'base' is flat, the protruding neck – and additional padlock – can make sitting less comfortable. Using plastic tags or (marked) cable ties can however alleviate a little of this awkwardness, depending on the compassion of the person in control.

Just as infibulation and the placing of piercings in a foreskin can limit access to the penis and its use, so piercing can be used as a means of anal control. Some may regard this as extreme, while others see such control as another – separate or additional –form of chastity, as transferring 'control of the hole' to another can be very powerful and very intimate.

The most effective technique is for ring piercings to be placed at the 'top' and 'bottom' of the sphincter. These are set about a centimeter – or just less than half an inch – deep through the flesh rather than through the 'ring muscle' itself. Each 'tunnel' or hole is probably no more than a centimeter long. A ball closure ring is put through each. While this may, at first, appear unhygienic, the very generous blood flow to the area – because of the rectum's function as a chamber in which liquid can be absorbed – accelerates healing. Those whose diets reduce the likelihood of constipation should have no difficult 'shitting as normal'. Wiping with toilet tissue make take a little more time and care than before but is generally sufficient for achieving necessary cleanliness. While a bidet, or sitting in a bathtub, may be extra helpful, not everyone has either. Having sanitary 'wipes' – produced for people with haemorrhoids – readily available is probably worthwhile too, especially during the healing period. It is important to note that this is a fairly specialist piercing and finding a professional piercer who has sufficient medical knowledge to be able to carry out the procedure and be willing to do it may not be at all easy.

But, yes, just having two rings here does not represent chastity in itself. So, how is penetration prevented? The two piercing rings have to be attached together. One way, although not necessarily particularly practical, could be to link the two bead-capture rings together. However, the disadvantages of this are, firstly, that the procedure would have to be done relatively frequently to keep potential mess to a minimum and, secondly, that doing so would gradually loosen the rings and increase the likelihood that a capture bead could be dislodged. Losing such beads can be inconvenient and irritating – and unlikely to enhance this particular experience. Therefore, alternatives should be considered.

The first is probably the use of a small padlock, but again – for reasons of hygiene and practicality – this would best be removed before the locked guy is allowed to shit. Keeping a padlock through a chastity cage or penis piercing clean can be difficult enough, doing so between the cheeks of the butt would be more time consuming and difficult. Therefore the most practical suggestion for keeping such rings attached together for reasonable periods of time – usually a few days at the most – would be a small, plastic cable tie. While these can be removed quickly and easily by the wearer – which is probably an advantage in case of any emergency – they can be marked by those in control so they become 'tamper proof'. Keeping the area clean is less difficult too, especially during bathing or directing a shower on to the area. Douche hoses can be used for this sort of external cleanliness too. Strips of plastic can also be wiped reasonably easily and effectively with toilet tissue. Such cable ties can then be adjusted so that the hole can expand enough to allow shitting while being tight enough to prevent either penetration by anything other than a relatively small hose and certainly not more than one or two (small) fingers, let alone any sizeable plugs, dildos, a strap-on or another man's penis.

CLEANLINESS

Like so many aspects of chastity, cleanliness requires thought. Every guy is different – and the trials and tribulations of keeping clean are very individual.

Basic cleanliness can be achieved by directing a shower nozzle directly at the device – and into a cage as fully as possible, usually at least once a day. In bathrooms where showers have been plumbed in, this may be impossible. An alternative may be to buy one of the plastic devices designed for attaching to taps or faucets for hair washing. Some men use the douche hoses they have attached to their showers.

For many using cage devices rather than full belt designs, the arrival of inexpensive liquid soaps on the supermarket shelves has been a blessing. Running the soap into the 'top' of a device or even squirting some into a piss slit opening has made personal hygiene far easier than it used to be. Everybody – and every body – can react differently to such products, so finding one that doesn't cause discomfort when applied to a sensitive part of the body is probably advisable. Some brands may be more astringent than others, but the anti-bacterial varieties should help reduce any unpleasant dampness and smelliness, especially for men with foreskin. If a product seems to sting when used neat, then dilute it and put the weaker solution into another container with a pump or similar dispenser. Let the soap stay in place for a few moments and then rinse it out thoroughly with water from a shower. Moving a device – and its contents – around vigorously in a bath can also rinse the soap away. Cotton buds can be used to get to difficult-to-reach places inside a cage too.

Astringent 'sanitizing hand gels' should probably be avoided – as they can contain an alcohol – unless causing discomfort is a consentual part of the interaction between the wearer and keyholder. (For some guys, the sensation can be quite intense and not unlike using products such as muscle 'balms' on the sensitive skin of the penis or scrotum.)

An alternative is to immerse a locked device – or the entire genitals – into a container of either salt water or a mild soap solution. Common sodium salt – which is sold most cheaply in many places as cooking salt – can be dissolved most easily and quickly in heated water, which should be allowed to cool before immersion! Alternatively, sit in a bathtub. Diluting a very small amount of salt or a medicated disinfectant into the water can be helpful too. Some guys have reported that they find the chlorine in swimming pools very worthwhile – an approach which has, they say, to be balanced by the possibility of devices being noticed, even under big and baggy swimwear.

Running liquid soap into the penis tubes of full belt devices such as the Goethals heavy, Carrara, Latowski or a Neosteel is possible – but rinsing and drying may be more time consuming. Some guys say sitting in a bathtub is more effective than using a shower, while others argue the opposite – because a shower head is more easily directed into difficult to reach areas. For belts that push the balls to each side, drying between the sac and the pubic area can be difficult. For cages, getting rid of any remaining dampness from the sac behind a penis tube may need particular care and attention. Cloth towels may be too thick, so facial and toilet tissues or absorbent paper towels sold for kitchen use may be easier to get into such places.

Some guys like to use talcum powder while others abhor that idea. Every locked guy has no real choice but to be patient while they experiment to find out what is most effective for them.

For guys in some designs of full belts, anal cleanliness requires extra assiduousness too. Some use side chains – like jockstraps – while others have single steel bands that run between the buttocks. One design includes an elliptical opening, however making sure that this is in exactly the right position for defecation can be testing. Everyone shits differently too. The consistency varies according to short and long-term diet and fecal sizes reflect the condition of the sphincter.

Pulling a single steel band to one side may be relatively straightforward, but other designs can potentially be more messy. Clearly, the most practical approach to cleanliness is to use a bidet, but they are not a universal bathroom or toilet fitting, especially in public restrooms! Even then, using plenty of toilet tissue is usually necessary first. Being able to step into the shower immediately after shitting can be preferable, using the head to direct water at the cleft between the buttocks to make sure that both that area of the body and the metal are fully clean.

Some factors are, clearly, more obvious than others. Circumcision has, for thousands of years, been a relatively straightforward approach to penile cleanliness; if a guy doesn't have a foreskin, then nothing can accumulate between it and the glans. Techniques, such as pulling the foreskin closed and using (fresh) urine to rinse the glans, can be impossible if the entire penis is locked away.

Uncut guys will have to assess for themselves how often they may need to be unlocked for cleaning. Those with tight foreskins may well need to be unlocked more often. Circumcision as an adult, with the surgery performed privately for either cosmetic or religious reasons, may be an expensive procedure – adding significantly to the already considerable cost of some chastity devices.

Men who seek medical attention, reporting that the foreskin is too tight or painful when retracted may find that surgery can be prescribed, so that the cost of the procedure is covered insurance or by other healthcare systems.

For men who are circumcised when they are more aware of their cocks, the glans may, at first, be so unusually sensitive that being locked is far more frustrating than for those who were circumcised soon after birth.

Technological developments can make supervision of unlocking easier for distance keyholders than ever in the past. Even without revealing anyone's face, someone can unlock, wash the genitals in a bowl of water while being monitored online, but, obviously, care is needed whenever liquid is anywhere near any electronic device.

Ambient and body temperatures are clearly factors affecting perspiration for everyone, but they become more acute for guys who are locked. Some men report that their skin cannot breathe and the airflow is not as great in silicon devices and that they become sweatier – and potentially smellier – more quickly in those devices than others.

CLOTHING

Work attire in particular clearly needs consideration. Clearly, bulkier devices are less likely to be obviously visible under baggier clothing. Some guys may find they have to sit with their legs further apart than usual while wearing the cup-like Carrara devices, so the posture and the bulge becomes more apparent without the cover of an office desk. Those who need to change into workwear may prefer the relative discretion of a smaller cage while others willingly show off their devices, even being brazen in communal showers.

Retailers say that most underwear for men is bought by women, which reflects a depressing indication of how most men regard their genitalia and genital comfort. Social attitudes towards the cock and balls – and the denial that surrounds them, illustrated by the plethora of euphemisms that exist in many languages, do not promote genital comfort. That some words for the male genitalia – such as 'junk' for example – are themselves also quite derogatory is not encouraging.

Men who are exploring chastity – whether selfishly or as aspect of interaction with a partner – will probably be less reserved in thinking about or trying different styles of underwear than others. Those coming to chastity anew may face having to confront their existing psychological conditioning, simply because they are more openly thinking about and talking about their genitals, so finding the style of underwear that is most appropriate for them individually may be part of this process too.

Underwear for men comes in two very basic forms; it is either supportive or it is not. Supportive underwear lifts the balls in some way – and the extent to which this happens and the effectiveness each depend very much upon the size, the cut and the material. The designs vary greatly too – from a miniscule thong (with a piece of thread running between the legs from the pouch between the buttocks to a narrow waistband), a jockstrap with back 'straps' at each side of the buttocks and, more often, a wider waistband, to trunks, boxer briefs, briefs and 'bikini' briefs. Trunks, most often, include a pouch but extend down the thigh. Boxer briefs also have pouches but are 'square cut', sitting on the hips and ending roughly parallel with the buttocks. Briefs are cut away so that the leg seams follow the line of the divide between the torso and the legs. The width of the sides can range between about two and six inches (5-15 centimeters) while bikini briefs are cut more narrowly, with sides rarely broader than two inches or five centimeters.

Boxer shorts are just that; shorts that are not at all supportive and baggy, which are either cut so that the genitals hang above the split between the legs or down one side. The original designs were based on the very baggy shorts worn by boxers – but under which the pugilists wore heavy leather padded 'guards' protecting their genitals.

Supportive underwear is produced in two distinctive – but frequently unrecognized – styles. Those from the US are designed so that the cock points downwards, laid on top of the balls, which seem to be pushed back between the legs. Most chastity devices are designed so that the cock points downwards to some degree – otherwise urination would either be impossible or horrendously messy. Many styles from Europe are intended to be worn with the balls pulled forward and the cock 'up' or to one side above the balls.

Pulling a locked cock upwards, in a European supportive style may not be at all comfortable – so a more American alternative, which lifts the balls and cage a little while keeping the locked cock in its downwards-pointing position, could be best. Men accustomed to the support and constraint these styles provide will probably have to get used to 'dressing' in a different way. That said, supportive underwear – of either design – is more likely to lift the genitals, so they do not bounce backwards and forwards as a man walks or they are lifted out of the way so they are not crushed between the legs when he sits down. Looking at designs carefully and some experimentation is probably the best approach for most guys.

Today's cotton material general retains its shape and strength – as long as it is not put carelessly through the laundry and exposed, unnecessarily, to the destructive tendencies of a tumbler drier. The wool of old did not have the strength to provide much support, so the effectiveness of underwear has increased in line with the material science that has led to the evolution of materials such as artificial fibres such as polyester and Spandex/Lycra, microfibers and even bamboo.

Cotton is said to 'breathe' and allow the skin to breathe more than artificial fibres but, with the addition of a small percentage of an elastic material such as polyester or Spandex, its supportive efficiency is greatly enhanced.

The advent of mass-produced, off-the-shelf, ready-to-wear pants and trousers also has to be taken into account. When, in the late 19th and early 20th centuries, affluent men had their suits made to measure by their tailors, they would be asked 'how they dressed', or whether their genitals flopped to the right or the left. In the 21st century, young men (probably very uncomfortably) wear baggy boxer shorts under jeans that are cut high between the legs, leaving them with genitals that are constrained, if not supported, by the denim.

'Suspensory bandages' – pouches attached to a waistband that lift the ball sac but provide 'freedom' (relatively speaking) for the cock – have also been suggested as being good for locked guys, as they provide some support for the balls while not constraining the cage at all.

So, what is best for someone in chastity? Some may prefer to have their locked genitals bouncing around without support – while others prefer the great comfort that comes from the material lifting the cage as well as their genitals up from between their legs. The choice has to be individual – and based probably on trial and error. However, thinking about outerwear is important too. Those who prefer wearing jeans may find that baggier, looser fitting designs are more comfortable – and draw less attention to the area between their legs – than tighter styles. Similarly, if you're going to wear a suit while you're locked, wear the device when you're going to try on a suit.

Trouser – pants – designs also vary between Europe and the US. Go in to most clothing stores in the US and the crotch will probably be cut lower than those on sale at the other side of the Atlantic. This is a probably a legacy of the tradition of baggy cotton boxer shorts being more commonplace and for a longer period of time. Men who have more hanging between their legs as a consequence of being locked in chastity may find that US styles are better than those found elsewhere.

Many locked guys have contributed to online discussions about what is best for them. One advocated the support of briefs while another said he preferred a thong made from a stretchy material. 'It allows the device to move a little and the fabric covers the testicles completely and reduces pinching,' he wrote. Another chose microfibre, saying: 'It has the right stretch for my cages and is smooth and comfortable. My cotton bikini briefs seem to rub weirdly on my sac.'

If discretion is important, said another, 'I would wear compression shorts to hold the cage pointing town with briefs over them to mask lumps.'

One guy said he chose underwear depending on which device he was wearing. In one full belt, he wore briefs and a proprietary brand of sanitary towel, intended for incontinence, to catch any drips, while in another he wore tighter designs.

Clearly, work clothing has to be comfortable while wearing a device, regardless of whether you're a truck driver, office worker or a bicycle courier. In his online FAQs, Aarkey suggested that, if your regular clothing doesn't fit particularly well, 'do what I did'. He went shopping wearing his chastity device – and bought 'leg wear' that allowed a little more room so the profile of the device was less obvious. Also, he said that he had had to think about being comfortable while sitting for long periods, especially while driving.

Almost every device will create its own profile under relatively tight-fitting swimwear, regardless of whether this is a brief Speedo-like design, a 'square-cut' short or a longer 'jammer' style. Consequently, baggier shorts are likely to provide greater camouflage. Some men say that the inner brief lining is enough to stop devices moving about too obviously while others prefer a second, tighter, layer to reduce a more pronounced bulge. The (large) Curve design can, obviously, be the most difficult to disguise and while, for example, the CB-2000 may be much smaller, like the Exobelt, the 'harder edges' of the tube can be noticeable. The more anatomical designs of others in the CB range or silicone alternatives may be most practical.

Some guys have expressed preferences for various styles of women's underwear – but the fundamental physical differences between male and female genital anatomy would suggest that designs for the female form are likely to allow far less space for any chastity device than a pouch of any size or shape. The appeal is, therefore, probably far more psychological than practical.

COMMUNICATION

Trying to achieve mutual and equitable candor while protecting and maintaining the dynamics seems to be a particularly sensitive and sometimes difficult aspect of establishing and preserving a power relationship – not least because communication can be so difficult for any of us whenever we are confronted by intimacy of one sort of another.

Cultural mythology would have us belief that a dominant can magically enter the mind of the submissive and know all there is to know without any exchange between them. Both may have read widely, be intelligent individuals and have thought long and often about their own needs and wants, apparent strengths and shortcomings. However, as soon as one bows his head to the other, assumption can quickly overtake actuality.

Introducing chastity to a relationship requires great sensitivity (see Relationships below). One man asked online how, as a highly-sexed recently-married young husband, he could introduce chastity as his wife did not seem to enjoy penetrative sex or fellatio and that she preferred vibrators to his (generous) endowment. The first respondent suggested that he was approaching the situation from his perspective, rather than hers and this needed to change first. 'If you want her to open up,' this person said, 'she will need to see how it benefits her, rather than you getting off. She should, he suggested, be the priority and then she may reciprocate with some interest.

The respondent went on to suggest that the wife needed evidence of his trust – which could be through handing the key *and* control. 'It will take time,' he added, 'and she will decide how comfortable she feels.' He then suggested taking her on a dream date, pampering her, doting on her. 'Talk about desires and fantasies,' he advised, 'but take it slow if she is shy or inexperienced; let her make discoveries rather than saying you want a, b and c', adding that this guy should ask her what she would like, be open, accept her choices and go at her pace, rather than his. And, he concluded, if she wants to keep that key and not use … for longer than you want, let her. You will, he said, soon follow her around like a puppy desperate for a treat, as his dominant tells him that he turns into a different person when he is locked. Such dedication really is about putting another person first, letting their plans and wishes have priority, letting them make the decisions, such as choosing where to go on a date or vacation. If you're already doing that, then adding more may be challenging. Express appreciation for whatever is done; be grateful for the smallest attention. If, the guy said, the man is only gets a hand job, thank her for that and let her know that his next orgasm, even a week away, will be hers to 'grant and give'. You need, he advised, to show that you're serious to get past any shyness.

Look at chastity websites, and most questions seem to come from guys wanting to be locked wondering how they can introduce the topic to relationships with male partners, wives or girlfriends. Far fewer come from potential keyholders keen to lock others. A rare, but consequently fascinating, conundrum came from a woman who wanted to lock her husband. Her account suggested that she was the more sexually imaginative and while he had been 'impassive' to kink, he had not refused altogether. 'I like him,' she said, 'when he is horny. He is delightful and attentive and I think it's time to introduce him to chastity.' She then sought suggestions from others who had faced similar situations with their partners and asked: 'What were some little steps to help him discover he will like this? I have not approached him on this topic yet, so he's a clean slate.'

While some responses were quickly slapped down as facile, the responses were largely mature, sensible and helpful. The first said: 'Chastity is about communication', before asking if the man was submissive. If he wasn't, the respondent said, the chances of him getting into it were poor. He suggested using a polycarbonate CB device for just a few hours at a time, while 'teasing the shit out of him' and making the reward after denial 'extra special', adding: 'The more pleasure you bring him, the more he will be willing to jump.'

Another suggested a trial period based on trust – but with incentives, such as 'getting a very nice surprise' after a week of no orgasms or genital touching. Another was more direct, suggesting: 'The best way to find out ... is to ask him then talk about it; no games, no forcing it on him.' A third thought a reward would be good from the starting point of 'if you try it, we can ...' which is something you know he likes. A fourth said simply, 'tell him how sexy it would be for you to have him wearing a cage and how it would turn you on' and let him discover how your body responds even to just talking about it.

That elicited the idea of explaining how he will be excited all the time and probably get more sex than before while yet another suggested getting him to read chastity stories as a way of assessing his interest. The consensus seemed to be that he would need more attention and arousal – while simultaneously being restricted from orgasms – so that his horniness and enthusiasm would increase. Get him to focus on making you happy, said another from a perspective of his own experience of being teased and exploited.

Simplicity was again suggested, using a comment such as: 'I really love it when you're horny, so no jerking off before date night or whatever ...' while another said that, for this potential keyholder, the best time to broach the subject was when the guy was being edged. 'I'll agree to just about anything at that point,' he admitted.

Realism was advocated too. 'Start with an open discussion,' said another man, 'at a time when you are both relaxed and just sitting together. Let him know the idea really turns you on and you have no intention of making him do anything he doesn't want to do.' Let him have control, have the lock to any device you get, and say he can decide when, or even if, he hands over the key.'

The woman who posed the original question did provide some feedback – saying that she had suggested some denial play when the guy got home from a business trip.

After that, another man added to the exchange – advising against an open discussion. He said he would not have agreed if a dominant had suggested it, as 'my thinking was why the hell should I give up my orgasms?' However, the dominant proposed short teasing periods with feedback emphasizing the enjoyment. He loved how it affected his brain and how the frustration was also fun and rewarding. However, he also said: 'Do not name it constant.' That changed it from 'fun anticipation' to 'just sucks', also, he added: 'Periods of freedom let the guy get used to ejaculating and producing, so when that freedom is taken away, it is all the more devastating.'

Power relationships are riddled with paradoxes. Particular challenges can be encountered during illness – as when a sub's perception of an omnipotent Dominant may be dashed by a virulent influenza virus. Alternatively, a dominant may appear to have to reverse the roles to nurse an ill submissive, calling on the sub to remember that it is the dominant's obligation to take care of the submissive, even to the extent of being a nursemaid rather than a leather-clad flagellant! Achieving the most for both from an interaction where the diametric opposites met to spark off each other and be greater than the sum of the two parts is not easy and should never be taken for granted.

The respect has to be mutual: the (supposed) submissive who says 'I've been in chastity for 20 minutes now for you' is not likely to be appreciated or welcomed back just as the dominant who makes too many assumptions too quickly about the power transfer may never see that submissive again.

So, how do you communicate in a way that reduces the likelihood that either will have less regard or respect for the other, whatever the adopted roles? Relationship counsellors say that we frequently fail to communicate because we never find the 'right time' to be as open as we want to be with someone close. We are afraid of catching them in the wrong mood at the wrong moment, being abrupt and then making matters worse rather than resolving any perceived problems or difficulties.

Setting specific times for such open communication is a good start. If you know you're going to be talking at, say, 10am on a Saturday, then you can prepare yourself for that. You know to get other anxieties out of the way and avoid potential distractions, such as phones and computers. You can find private space and, while the sub may still call the keyholder 'Sir' or 'Ma'am' and be called 'boy' or whatever, each can respect the other's honesty and emotions.

Alternatively, if maintaining the roles in open conversation is too difficult, write to each other. Again, the (gay) 'leather' world has long advocated that submissives should keep journals which their tops can read. This is good, but it only goes one way and half the way. In such situations, the top should also document their feelings. Just as therapy groups often agree from the outset that 'what is said in this room stays in this room', so a similar agreement is essential before adopting this technique. Complete honesty is essential too; if you're pissed off with the other because of something, does the irritation actually originate in that behavior? Or is the exasperation misdirected because it was actually provoked by something elsewhere, such as an incident at work or outside the house?

Don't try to do this too often, especially at first, because the initial enthusiasm is likely to dissolve quite quickly and the practice will be abandoned. Rather than weekly, try making such exchanges every month or so; time – and deep breaths – can put annoyances into perspective. Remember too that misdirected anger is inappropriate and unhealthy anger.

A third approach is to involve a mutual acquaintance, preferably someone who is known about equally by both and who has an appreciation of the dynamics of a power relationship. If this person has counselling skills, so much the better.; if they don't their interest in you, what you're doing and trying to achieve, may be the incentive they need to try to learn more for themself. Often trying merely to describe a frustration, putting feelings into words is itself therapeutic. (It can explain why prayer or writing a letter can be so effective or the origin of the expression that a problem shared is a problem halved.)

Locked57 has also provided guidance on being 'a good locked guy', the core of which is communication. He advises taking care of your body and your device – but then sticking to the agreement that has been reached with a keyholder, keeping in regular contact and reporting not only any lapses but providing feedback about your emotions and what you are experiencing psychologically as well as physically.

Silence equals miscommunication and simultaneously militates against the success of any chastity or power relationship. Those involved forget that at their peril.

CONTROL AND POWER TRANSFER

For many men, chastity and control are synonymous and symbiotic; one cannot exist without the other while both are mutually inclusive and important.

Only one variable exists for them – and that is whether the chastity is just one aspect of greater control or whether the control is limited to chastity alone.

In this context, defining control is probably vital at the outset. For these purposes, the essence is probably best described as being the transfer of any aspect of choice, and consequent decision-making, over any feature or portion of another person's life and the way he lives. Some have come to call this the *exchange* of power, while others consider the term *power transfer* to be more accurate and honest – as the action is primarily one way, from the locked guy to the keyholder.

Few, if any, relationships that involve power transfer are the same; the degree and intensity of the control varies greatly. In each, the extent to which the decision-maker, *the dominant*, exercises influence or control over the other, the *submissive*, has to be determined. Some dominants like to allow submissives scope to use their imaginations, to use their intelligence and intellect to observe the dominant, to learn enough about his traits and behaviors so that they can each anticipate his needs. Others are more strict, more intense.

Some refer to this as micro-management, where constraints are imposed of far more aspects of the submissive's existence. These may, for example, include limits to the extent of communication – setting parameters to when a submissive may speak or the range of specific words, terms or sentences that may be used. Alternatively, the parameters may include clothing, personal appearance, posture and deportment, the use of domestic facilities, exercise and diet.

The parameters may themselves vary according to situation – with one set applying to the dominant and submissive in private, another to them being together in public with others relating to the submissive when he is apart from the dominant, either in private or in public.

The (probably simultaneous) processes of extending control over a submissive or during which he becomes familiar with the power transfer, can be described as *training*. While the nature of the relationship per se may be a great motivator for the submissive, the formality of power transfer is undermined if breaches are not accompanied by sanctions of some sort while achievements should balance the 'stick-and-carrot' approach with reward.

The library of non-fiction material covering aspects of training is relatively limited. Some has started to show its age – such as Larry Townsend's *Leatherman's Handbook*. Guy Baldwin's *Complete Slave* offers some suggestions while the homoerotic guides written by Jack Rinella have much to commend them. *The Control Book* by Peter Masters, for instance, is weakened by an absence of a strong foundation in psychology. He gives the impression of writing from the perspective of a 'practical' top – without understanding the mind of the submissive.

The origins of submission can be seen in the behavior of a child seeking affection or approval. The perspective of the eminent psychologist Erik Berne, documented in the much-cited work *Games People Play*, can provide a helpful and practical context. His concept of transactional analysis, and the further exploration of his ideas by Thomas A Harris in his later book *I'm OK; You're OK* are probably worthwhile reading for any dominant wishing to explore power transfer 'for real', whatever the level of intensity. In the Berne context, the dominant can be regarded as the parent while the submissive is the child, but a mature child. Berne's approach can help both dominant and submissive answer the question: 'what does anyone seek in submission?'

The answer probably lies in a mutual exchange of responsibilities, perhaps simplistically expressed as 'I'll look after you if you'll look after me'. The dominant assumes the role of provider, of hunter-gatherer while the submissive is the protected purveyor of domestic comfort. Sex may be a great motivator – but the dynamic can encompass far more aspects of life and living, such as sleep, food, water, and a home. Simultaneously, the distinction between use and *ab*use is very narrow and variable, according to mood, temperament and circumstances.

A parent raises a very dependent child to be self-dependent to the point of independence, a temporary period of life before the offspring undergoes a metamorphosis into parenthood and faces additional burden of dependent elders.

In the 21st century, any transfer of power should observe and respect another person's inane human rights, even though the dynamic may, for example, include aspects of objectification, infantilism and or 'animal play' (whereby someone explores, literally and metaphorically, their 'inner puppy'.)

However, fiction has much to offer. Clearly some writing is romanticized (in more ways than one) while other authors describe situations which are clearly entirely impractical or violent and abusive beyond the extent of all but the most extreme dimensions of consent. The fictional approach often involves the separation of the submissive from 'every day life' for a period, something that may not be possible for those who have to earn a living for themselves. However, relatively recent writings – such as *The Trainee* by Tom Henderson or *Training Alex* by Jacob Morrison – describe some methods, such as constraints on expression and so on, which could be adapted and adopted within the realities of working lives.

Both, to a limited extent, also raise – and consider – the potential dangers of dependency; when a submissive has been so protected or controlled by a dominant that life is disproportionately and potentially destructively challenging should anything happen to the dominant. This may appear extreme, but the need for this to be acknowledged and considered increases in direct ratio to the extent to which power is being transferred.

Additionally, within the context of control, the terms *sanctions* or *penalties* are probably preferable to *punishment* – as, for example, a beating may be a very exciting (sexual) experience which is more appropriate when used as positive reinforcement and a reward rather than as a deterrent.

The most powerful positive or negative motivators for each of us are established very early in our lives, during our conditioning; our formative years. To exert greatest control, the dominant should strive to identify these within the submissive. They may not correspond to his own particular turn-ons but, once identified, they can be exploited to mold the submissive towards these. By identifying his own, he can also then pass this information to the submissive – who, within the permitted parameters of being imaginative and creative, brings this knowledge to bear in the way he strives to please and serve the dominant.

For example, a dominant may consider that a submissive should never wear underwear – but the submissive has an underwear fetish. The dominant may exploit this by restricting the circumstances when underwear is permitted or allowing it as a reward. Alternatively, a submissive may be averse to anything feminine – while this is exciting to the dominant; either because of the physicality per se or because the submissive is being challenged. The slow process towards reaching a mutually exciting compromise could be broached through, for instance, the use of 'manscara' or exceedingly brief bikini underwear or hosiery specifically designed and marketed for men; a strategy that could preclude revulsion and potential rejection.

Similarly, if a submissive knows that such behaviors may arouse and please a dominant, and that 'better' sex may result, he may metaphorically take a deep breath and make the effort as a gesture of his submission and a genuine expression of his desire to serve and please.

One very important aspect of control is that it must be exercised – in many senses of that word. For a locked guy who transfers any aspect of choice over his life and the way he lives to another, the reassurance that this is being done is exceedingly important.

If, for example, monitoring of any sort is agreed, then just as the locked guy is under an obligation to the relationship to provide the necessary information, the keyholder enters into the arrangement by agreeing to provide some supervision. Evidence that this is being done is a mutual obligation and pact.

Technology offers benefits in these situations too. Those involved can create a free e-mail account – which usually includes a calendar function. If both have the password(s), the locked guy can use this to report in while the keyholder can carry out the necessary checks. Nothing can be more demoralizing or potentially undermine a relationship or a locking agreement if a locked guy who has religiously been spending time and effort contributing to such a protocol discovers that the keyholder hasn't even bother to look at what is being provided, especially if this is discovered after a period of some weeks.

The keyholder may, perhaps even should, make random checks, perhaps two or three times in one day and then not again for, say, a week so that the locked guy is not tempted to become lax. The keyholder may not provide feedback immediately, but perhaps – over a period that is relevant within busy lives – makes comments on the detail or timing of contributions some days apart.

Control and consent are also inextricably linked. Each dimension needs to be identified, negotiated and agreed. The resulting compact, if not contract, should be written and, depending on the technology and distance involved, mutually endorsed. The who, what, where, when, and how dimensions are obviously most important. If those involved wish to achieve greater intimacy, adding the reasons why, perhaps as a codicil to the document, could be fascinating and valuable. The exercise, in which the (written) results are shared with the other, could be a psychological powerful (and potentially very liberating) method of self-analysis and personal disclosure.

Doing so may appear to be translating the sexual into the bureaucratic (for those who don't already enjoy such perversions, of course), but drawing up a grid so that the dimensions can be identified and discussed may be helpful. If the keyholder and locked guy are not geographically close together, this can be sent backwards and forwards by e-mail or the details can be discussed and then entered during an online chat or telephone conversation. The result can form the basic of the written agreement for them.

Although control may be extended to much of a submissive's life, eroticism frequently remains all-important. Control is also amazingly intimate. A locked guy can be walking along and suddenly remember the device around his genitals; he can remember the person who holds the key. Similarly, the keyholder can suddenly remember that somewhere, perhaps half a world away, he has the power to determine when another man may, or may note, touch a vital part of his anatomy. The physicality of chastity keeps them in each other's thoughts.

This, however, is only half of the dynamic; the other half is telling each other. Technology has made that far easier and practical. Messaging software for smartphones means that short messages can be sent from one continent to another almost instantaneously and very affordably. Reminding one another of the predicament of each can increase intimacy beyond measure, event over huge distances and many time zones. Such communication can be controlled too – but not destructively, by imposing too intense constraints on frequency and amount while (limited) denial can be used as a punishment.

Like so much in life, problems around control seem to emerge – and become unnecessarily destructive – when communication is insufficient, both at the start and then after that. Candor is vital, with self analysis probably preceding disclosure and negotiation. Just as chat should precede chastity, it should precede control.

DRYNESS

Ensuring dryness after bathing or showering may not be straightforward. Some guys suggest pushing tissue paper of some sort into the device to try to get rid of lingering drops of water. Others recommend dripping a little baby oil or silicon lube into a tube first – so that water is displaced. Another recommendation has been using talcum powder – although some may find this a little messy and unsightly.

EDGING

Edging is the idea of getting close to (the edge of) orgasm and then stopping sexual stimulation. The intention is that horniness is increased – but without release.

Locked57 has suggested that keeping another guy aroused and 'on edge' lessens the likelihood that chastity will become boring for either the keyholder or a locked guy.

Learning how to 'read' a man so that stimulation can cease as close as possible to ejaculation or orgasm is an acquired skill. For many men, learning how to read themselves also requires attention and concentration in a way they would otherwise ignore.

Some cultures promote the idea of 'coitus reservatus' – where the intention is to remain at the 'plateau' of penetration for as long as possible without ejaculating. Some call this 'karezza', from the Italian, but the activity or technique has also been described as a 'controlled sexual union' which is, apparently, not the same as 'orgasmic brinkmanship', another phrase used to describe edging.

The term karezza was coined by 19th century obstetrician and gynaecologist Alice Stockham – who also believed that men took between two weeks and a month to recover from every ejaculation and who advocated that, unless procreation was the aim, then the 'final propagative orgasm should be entirely avoided'. Alice was an advocate of women's rights – and promoted karezza as a way in which men should treat women 'decently'. Much to the chagrin of some religious fundamentalists, she promoted lovemaking as harmonious, leading to 'sublime spiritual delights', and allowing women and men who can achieve anal orgasms to reach several climaxes during a single act of penetration.

Occultist Alisteir Crowley also devised the concept of *erotocomatose lucidity* in 1912 – as a ritual that uses repeated stimulation (but not orgasm) to get someone into a state between being awake and asleep at the same time as being totally exhausted as a route to divine communication. Some followers of this philosophy promote eventual orgasm while others argue that exhaustion itself is the preferable trance-like state. Crowley also apparently intended that any semen – or 'elixir' – should be consumed, a suggestion which has been interpreted as an alternative to vampirism. A solo version requires repeated masturbation, to ejaculation, as a route to similar exhaustion.

ELECTRO

Technology's intrusion into everyday living for so much of humanity has even reached chastity. Such additions are not cheap – adding further expense to an interest that can, at least initially, require a 'considered' investment.

Electro sex per se – can involve sensations that range from the very gentle and deliciously sensuous to the exceedingly intense and, yes, definitely painful. While most 'smaller' devices are specifically designed for stimulating the genitals, they can also be used to deliver current to single or bipolar butt plugs and to the nipples. Generally, physicians and many experienced kinksters advocate great care when using electricity to stimulate the nipples while some avoid all such play above the waistline, because of the potential inter-reaction between the current and the natural electromagnetic field surrounding the heart. Some toys are available that run the current simply across each nipple, but some feel that if two are being used simultaneously, some current could nevertheless run across the chest. The greatest danger – which could be fatal – is of a current running across the heart as this can interfere with the heart muscle and playing with electricity, however weak the current may seem to be, in this way should be avoided altogether.

Some prefer to use electricity in ways that have been developed as part of physio- (or physical) therapy – to stimulate larger muscles, such as the glutes, abs and thighs. Such 'scenes' do however seem more suited to the physicality of much SM rather than the context of chastity and power dynamics. In this, pads – usually about four or five centimeters or an inch-and-a-half square – are attached to the skin above particular muscles, such as those in the upper back, the abdominals or thighs as electrodes.

'Zapping' the cock can, for example, be an amazing way for many men to achieve ejaculation and orgasm without either penetration or the need for any other physical contact – which may, at first, appear to be inconsistent with the denial of such sensations through chastity.

Some believe that the penis is not worth of stimulation that involves direct contact with the flesh of another person, especially within power relationships that include overt psychological interplay surrounding the size, purpose or value of the sub's (male) genitalia. This may be one-way or include comparison with aspects of the genitalia of the Dominant (regardless of gender). Intense electrical shocks can be used, whether or not a submissive male is in chastity or not, as a reminder of this.

For others, sensuous electrical stimulation of the submissive's cock may be a form of edging – bringing the guy towards a climax but then denying it after a period of stimulation. Such frustration may be a means to increasing and then achieving greater submission. Alternative, a more painful, sharp and brief shock may be used either as a punishment or as a form of control.

Electro sex has come a long way since the early, hand-cranked magnetos, used for military telephones, were used to generate (literally) very intense power. While these could be truly instruments of torture, as the voltage was greater than many (even strong, well-trained) men could tolerate and they were almost impossible to control, the sophistication of 'e-stim' units has increased steadily since the 1990s. Some must be linked directly to the electrodes by wires – while other remote control designs have become available.

The primary reason for combining electricity to chastity seems to be as a means for the dominant to increase control over the submissive. Some milder stimuli can be used as instructions; they are sufficient to attract the submissive's attention and specific combinations of stimuli can be designated as particular commands.

The two principle contact areas are the shaft or glans of the penis and the basic 'back' ring around the cock and balls – for those who are in cage devices – and/or the anus.

Electrostim units vary greatly in sophistication and, consequently, in price. The Erostek remote control unit – which can be used with some chastity devices but also in conjunction with other electrodes, was – in 2015 – available online from the manufacturers for approximately $400 (US) plus shipping and sales tax.

The disadvantage of using anal devices with some full belt designs that incorporate fixing mechanisms is that these can only be inserted or removed by taking off some or all of the belt. By 2015, the well-established European manufacturers of full belt designs – Latowski and Neosteel – had included variants that incorporated electrodes. Latowski had added electrodes to the genital chamber of his device – which could be controlled remotely. The electrodes for the shaft – which are not unlike those on electrical collars for training dogs – are powered by a rechargeable battery. One smaller unit, with a range of approximately 150 meters (or 165 yards) was available for about $650 (US) with variations according to shipping destinations and local taxes, while an altogether more powerful unit with a range of about 800 meters or about half a mile, was selling for about $700 in early 2015.

Latowski had also produced another device – powered by a 'Tens-like' unit with wires – that seemed more appropriate for arousal and edging and, Mario Latowski suggests, actually achieving orgasm while locked.

Although Walter Goethals does not specifically mention electro control on his Carrara website, his customization service does allow for the incorporation of such 'additions'.

With the main electrodes built in to the 'chamber' for the genitals and the receiver incorporated into the cup-like front of the belt, Mario Latowski's design does appear practical for use under clothing and, probably after experimentation to identify shock levels that communicate with the wearer without bringing his reactions to any unwanted attention from others, could well be used in many settings. While some couples may have sex lives that are limited, being able to remind someone in chastity that they are getting too far away while pushing a cart round a supermarket can add to the fun of the predicament – for both the guy who is locked and the keyholder.

The Neosteel addition is more limited – in that the electrode is a dildo attached to a bar between the cheeks and the receiver for a remote control unit is a small box that is placed against the base of the spine, above the waistline.

The most sophisticated electro additions for many devices are produced by Dream Lover Laboratories, which operate from an address in Hong Kong. While the ethos behind the development of the products is presented very much in the context of (dominant) women trying to (re-)establish control over primarily heterosexual males, the gender of the keyholder is actually irrelevant.

While the price of the most sophisticated device was – at 2015 rates – nearly $2,000 (US), they have encouragingly used the website to point out that one of the three products (at $would cost, over a two-year period, the equivalent of $58 per month; at $1.90 per day, about half the cost of a coffee from a leading global corporate chain which, they helpfully add: 'you can now save on, since your male will be enjoying a different type of "stimulant".'

The design appears very realistic – as it includes a waterproof receiver with a battery that can last for as long as three months. Unlike some others, 'the electrodes,' they say, 'do not need the application of special gels nor do they cause itching or discomfort.' Such features, the website adds, 'are crucial in obtaining true long-term compliance.'

The DreamLover 2000 system has a line-of-sight range of about 80 meters or slightly more than 200 feet – but about a quarter of that if the wearer's body is between the transmitter and receiver. The software has been designed for Mac, Windows and Android operating systems and includes a 'pager' function so that the wearer can be summoned as well as timed pulses and sensors that can detect any tampering and the effectiveness of the contact with the flesh. Another sensor can tell whether the wearer is standing upright – in 'learn' mode – or on all fours – 'canine' mode. The software can also tell when the wearer moves too far away from the local transmitter and the battery on the receiver is, the manufacturers say, easily recharged using a USB port. The technical specifications vary between the three models – the Lite, the Pro and the Pro Mobile – that were available and described on the website in early 2015.

Each model includes a receiver, remote control, electrodes and bounding parts, the USB interface, adaptor, batteries, waterproof waistband, a case and padlocks and a CD carrying the drivers, software, user guide and safety video. The Pro version also includes an 'arousal indicator'.

Of course, much of the effectiveness depends on the imagination of the users. For example, one man said online: 'Even better than a bitchy keyholder who doesn't allow release is one who also sadistically enjoys shooting electric shocks to those denied balls with a little remote control … because sometimes never being allowed to cum is not, in itself, sufficient suffering and humiliation.'

Another agreed, saying that just because the submissive is in public doesn't mean that the keyholder should abstain from delivering any shocks.

The range of devices that are available ready for use with electricity or which can relatively cheaply and easily be adapted so that electrodes can be added is increasing steadily. By 2015, they had includes both full belts from Goethals/Carrara and Neosteel as well as steel from Mature Metal and polycarbonate designs similar to the CB6000. The latest information should be found using your favorite search engine.

EMERGENCIES

The friend who first introduced me to a heavy metal belt had a substantial road motorbike – which he would ride while locked. He told of his astonishment when he had arranged, as a submissive, to spend some time serving a dominant man who happened to be a physician. The medic pointed out to him that, if he ever came off the bike and needed emergency surgery, getting him out of the device could delay any major operation by longer than the 'golden hour', so often crucial to survival. The steel would, the physician said, probably be too thick for the metal cutters found in most hospital emergency departments. Firefighters, he continued, would need to be called, with the heavyweight shears used to cut open cars. Apart from which, cutting an expensive device would ruin it forever. Wasn't there, he asked, any way of keeping a key with the wearer in case of such eventualities?

Personal experience strongly advocates the realities of safety. Only on the internet, one guy suggested, do you find fantasy posts about guys being locked up against their will or locked being damaged so cages can never be removed, even in a life and death situation. 'I learned my lesson,' he added, 'when I was rushed into surgery straight from my place of work. Luckily I had an emergency key because time was of the essence.'

My friend, who was a creative soul, put his imagination to work. His answer was to put the key in a separate, small, locket which he wore on a chain around his neck; breaking that open would probably take seconds or a minute or two at the very most. Destroying such a locket was, he thought, a very small price to pay to allow quicker hospital treatment – and not destroy an expensive device. The belt could be unlocked and removed within another minute or two – and rescued for the future. Any embarrassment factor would be no greater and, he confessed, he found that wearing the locket added further to the psychological dimension; freedom was simultaneously so close, and so obvious – as it could be easily seen if he opened a second button on a shirt or whenever he stripped to wash - while being totally out of reach. The reminders of his predicament each day added to the excitement for him and were almost as effective in maintaining his 'sexual enthusiasm' as edging.

Later, Tollyboy added a feature to the waistband that included an additional post through which an 'ordinary' padlock or plastic tag could be added. The rotary locks on the waistband and the front plate still provided the more intense security, but the extra 'check and balance' allowed the wearer to hold a key to those locks while either a plastic tag or small, cheaper, more easily destroyed padlock guarantee security while simultaneously allowing rapid escape in an emergency.

Padlocks can present problems too. I encountered a major predicament when I used one very well-known proprietary brand in the United States through a Prince Albert piercing. Within hours, it had seized and would not open. Fortunately, I was able to call a friend who lived a couple of blocks away whose roommate had large metal cutter. The roommate was a strong man but even he needed a fair amount of strength to cut through the hasp. Using a small metal saw would have taken hours and been difficult. The alternative would have been firefighters or the hospital emergency room. Fortunately, the roommate had kink interests too – and, while he was amused by my plight, he was sympathetic too otherwise the situation could have been embarrassing (not least for the stupidity in not having checked the lock before using it in that way).

Look for brass – that is less likely to corrode – than steel. If the finishing in steel is not particularly good and the metal is cheap, then one shower or one piss could be enough to make a small, inexpensive padlock impossible to open. Also, knowing whether you live in a hard or soft water area can be a factor too. More calcium in the water may – as 'furr' accumulates in kettles – build up in locks, so the frequency of lock cleaning should take this into account. Such factors may need to be considered when travelling too.

Breaking the hasp of a padlock, either with sufficiently strong metal cutters or a saw, or even trying to find scissors strong enough to cut a numbered plastic tag may also, in the most extreme circumstances, take longer than doctors would like.

Some guys suggest keeping a key in a block of ice in a freezer (at home), but emergencies can happen when you're not at home. Also, running the ice under a hot tap or trying to thaw it in a pan on a stove may not be practical either. (Putting metal into microwave ovens is generally not advised.)

Alternatively, combination devices have been recommended, especially where both the keyholder and locked guy have cell phones. However, this also relies on the keyholder being able to answer the phone or respond to a message. (And who hasn't found themselves somewhere where the battery has run down and they don't have a charger or other power?)

Most practical probably is for the locked guy to have a key in a sealed envelope that he can have with him at all times. Either he, or the keyholder, can put a mark – such as their signature or initials – across the seal so that the envelope becomes 'tamper proof'. A knowledgeable keyholder will appreciate and understand that the key will only be removed in a genuine emergency while the locked guy knows he will have to justify its removal.

Some keyholders and supervisors require evidence that the seal is in tact to be provided fairly frequently. Again, the use of smart phones with cameras makes this easy. Photographs can be taken at specified times – which should be recorded automatically in the metadata accompanying the image file – and sent immediately. While attaching pictures to text messages was, for a time, relatively expensive, internet messaging has reduced the cost considerably.

Using combination 'lock safes' is another possibility – but again probably they are best limited to situations where locked guys remain relatively close by and each keyholder can be contacted at all hours or the day or night by phone for the release code.

If a keyholder intends insisting on a padlock without recourse to an emergency key, then allowing the wearer to have heavy bolt cutters or a set of padlock shears (available from many leading hardware chain stores in many countries) is probably sensible.

ERECTIONS

From the questions and anecdotal accounts posted to various chastity websites, two particular issues seem to arise (if that's the appropriate word in this context) regarding erections. The first is the effect that chastity, particularly extended periods of being locked in a device, may have and the second regards comfort.

Some men have reported that erections seem to diminish in both strength and frequency the longer they are locked. The general idea seems to be that this starts to happen after about a month or six weeks as the brain appears to become conditioned to the predicament and the impracticality. (The impression is that strong erections do return after unlocking and the removal, especially of extremely constraining, devices – but this may take a few days, perhaps longer.)

As far as ease is concerned, a few guys report that discomfort, even pain, is a reminder of their predicament and should be endured as stoically as being locked per se. Others have pointed out that getting hard is less uncomfortable when they are clothed and wearing underwear helps keep the device pointing downwards. When naked – often in bed at night – they say that the longer the time that penis pulls the back ring of the device against the ball sac, stretching that and the more it is likely to cause chafing (along the perineum).

EXERCISE

For many locked guys, sports can present physical challenges. Heavy metal belt devices do not 'go well' with many contact sports for many reason. Also, despite the improvements to waistband designs over the years, especially the development of ergonomic waistbands by manufacturers such as Walter Goethals in Belgium and Neosteel in Germany, potentially serious chafing can occur.

(I remember jogging while wearing a Tollyboy belt. It hadn't been made especially for me, so the front panel was longer than a customized one would or should have been. The result was horrendous rubbing and soreness between the thighs that became unbearable after a couple of miles. I walked home.)

Read some of the anecdotal contributions to websites such as Fetlife and Lockedmen and it quickly becomes apparent that relatively few guys have difficulties exercising while being locked, but this also implies that they are selective about the ways that they keep fit. Assuming that they have consequently probably chosen cage designs, rather than full belts, seems reasonable, but generally the reports suggest that these too are not necessarily obstacles to physical fitness. Some guys clearly avoid team and contact sports which would bring them into close physical contact with others who may notice – and not necessarily appreciate – their predicament. Some, for the same reason, will avoid overt nudity and open changing facilities where devices may be seen, preferring instead to undress at home or in private.

Guys who like to swim suggest that the more pronounced bulge or angular profile of a device is less likely to be apparent in a baggy pair of shorts – with or without an inner brief – than in more tightly-fitting swimwear. Others enjoy the attention that comes with wearing a device at a 'clothing-optional' venues, such as nude beaches or at swimming sessions organized exclusively for gay men.

The additional bouncing and friction that can come with running for example could cause chafing, so using a little ointment in advance may be beneficial.

Some guys do not like their genitals moving very much at all while they are exercising, so they tend to choose the 'support' of tighter jockstraps or even Speedos under shorts, 'joggers' or sweatpants. For locked guys, these may put so much pressure on the back rings, for example, that they become uncomfortable, so a slightly looser jock may be preferable. Others do not worry at all about everything bouncing up and down as they run. As with swimming, the tighter the fit the greater the visibility, so anatomical devices may be better for some ... which logically leads to discussing:

'EXPOSURE'

Both keyholders and wearers do, it seems, get quite a thrill out of locking – or being locked – in ordinary, day-to-day circumstances where overt sexual behavior is conventionally out of place and where the wearer experiences the thrill of potential, if improbable, 'exposure'.

In an exchange on the Fetlife website in March 2015, one Domme started by saying that she loved seeing a guy in a steel device, especially worn under panties and trousers, and then asking whether any submissives had worn such devices under their suits while in the office.

One respondent immediately reflected potential business disadvantages though, saying: 'I have found that I should not wear it in heavy negotiating meeting as I tend to be softer (no pun intended) with my JailBird on' while another Dom said he regularly sent his 'daddy' to work in his.

Another respondent, presumably a man, added: 'In the past, I have worn a chastity device under my suit, and even when I have given speeches. I sometimes wonder whether anybody in the audience can notice!'

One guy said he was always locked while another said he was in a plastic, rather than steel, device and third confessed to wearing frilly, pink, lace, lingerie. The same person later added that he had worn suits, jeans, sweats, and skirts over the chastity device, but that he always wore panties as they felt 'so much better on than nasty men's shorts', adding: 'There is no comparison'. A fourth was more self-conscious, saying that while he had worn a device under a suit several times; when he started he 'had to refrain from looking down all the time to verify whether anything was visible as that would only attract attention.' Gradually, he continued, it 'became a habit' before confessing that 'it's harder to wear lacy panties'.

A submissive declared that he wore his device continually, during work and travel – a silicone Birdlock device with plastic numbered tags, adding that I 'never leave home without it'. For someone else, there was 'nothing like the feel of a cock-lock under panties' while another admitted that he was 'both locked up and in panties courtesy of my owner'. One man said: 'I'm too big for the plastic and silicone cages but I have worn one of the larger metal ones under a suit' adding the advice that 'it's definitely noticeable with flat-front pants but not so much with pleated'.

Another said he had worn his at the office every day for several years while a dominant said one locked sub had no option but to be locked a work as he was in a device all day every day. Others said that while they might not wear suits to work, they still wore their devices. One was more specific, revealing that he went into 'heavy negotiations' in a Looker 2 (from Steelworxx in Germany) but that he liked wearing a suit in the office as the cut provided more space while he implied that he went out to enjoy the nightlife, a device might potentially be more visible under tighter jeans. Someone altogether more brazen added: 'I should try out different kinds of suits and see which ones show the most' ....

As far as the 'profile' or how obvious a device may be, the Curve – from AL Enterprises – is one of the biggest. Consequently, pants or trousers need to have a low crutch so that it can 'hang' comfortably without becoming too pronounced or obvious. Harder metal and polycarbonate devices may also become obvious, but this largely depends on the tightness of outer clothing, the thickness of the fabric, the choice of underwear and the way the wearer is sitting or standing. Silicon devices are more pliable and can be crushed a little more easily, so that the outline may – if someone is looking closely – be apparent. The anatomical designs of many plastic and polycarbonate devices, to replicate the contours of the glans do mean that any protuberance may simply be regarded as that of a guy who is well-endowed. The outlines of others, however, may be no more or no less revealing than the shorts – and underwear – chosen by some sportsmen and athletes that may give those who are interested little doubt about whether they are, or are not, circumcised.

For some locked guys, decisions about exposure risks are included when they agree the 'dimensions of consent' with their keyholders. One gay man in his 20s, living in California, told me online that his dominant keyholder enjoyed knowing that his predicament could be known by others. He worked in a coffee shop in a cosmopolitan neighborhood of a large city, so his dominant restricted his clothing to very tight T-shirts that showed off his large nipples and very tight jeans, without any underwear, that did nothing to disguise the profile of his device. He was allowed to wear baggier shorts and a jockstrap when he went jogging, but was limited to very tight, brief swimwear at the nearby pool. His co-workers, he said, had quickly learned about the nature of the relationship, accepting him and his predicament warmly if, initially, with some bemusement. Some customers would spot his bulge, appreciate what was there and smile while regular swimmers had become so accustomed to him that they no longer took any notice.

FRUSTRATION (AND USE)

Some keyholders report that they like to 'experience' and 'use' the cocks they otherwise have locked away. (Clearly this involves dealing with preconceptions regarding penetration and power – which are mentioned elsewhere in this book.)

For some, such penetration may be very loving and intimate – with the (un-)locked guy finally allowed to achieve an ejaculatory orgasm. (However, as the sections on long-term locking and unlocking show, expecting a full and throbbing erection immediately after several weeks in a small device is probably being over-optimistic.)

Some keyholders – both men and women – have reported that they like using their (otherwise) locked men in a way that is almost dildo-like. They want the human penetration and the physical sensation that comes from having a real penis inside them and from having another body in contact with their own – but they still do not want the otherwise locked (submissive) guy to ejaculate. Online reports document the (basic) use of numbing creams – or lidocaine sold in US drugstores as a remedy for toothache – and several (layers of) condoms to reduce the sensitivity and sensuality of penetration. One man said he had read about a guy whose penis had been wrapped in electrical tape and three condoms before he was 'ridden' for two hours without cumming. The veracity of this is, of course, impossible to establish, but the anecdote illustrates the extremes to which some people think they may go. Also, some writers have suggested that this approach alone can extend the duration of penetrative intercourse while others have advocated using medications to overcome erectile dysfunction (such as Viagra) to enhance the pleasure for the person being penetrated and the frustration for the man whose penis is being used this way. (In such circumstances, the readily available warnings about the use – and mis-use – of such medications should be studied, and observed, carefully.)

Psychologically, the ambience of such activity could be very intimate and personal or alternatively provide an opportunity for those involved to explore aspects of objectification – but that is for them to decide.

GAMES

Combining chance with chastity appeals to some too, be they keyholders or locked guys. Games that do this can be appealing too – in addition to chastity per se. The 2014 Lockedmen website research revealed that 30 per cent of 900 respondents had played 'chastity bingo' at least once while others had used online and electronic tools – such as the Carlilock – to determine how long someone would be locked.

(However, those considering charging for keyholding services should probably note that this research revealed that fewer than 40 respondents said they had paid for such services – out of nearly 900 who answered that particular question, so chance may have a great appeal in that particular marketplace.)

As with so much, the only limits are those set by the imaginations of those involved. (Contributions for future editions of this book are welcome; a contact address is provided at the very end.)

At a kink event in the United States many years ago, my Tollyboy friend was locked. To be unlocked over the six days, he had to find the person holding the key. By the last morning, he was getting a little anxious, not least because he was due to go through airport security early the following day and, even in the early 1990s, he felt that doing that while locked in a substantial metal belt would guarantee unwanted or unnecessary attention. About 200 guys were gathered for brunch and one, a priest, stood and announced that the key was not being held by anyone sitting in the room at that time. He was telling the truth; it wasn't. *He* had the key and he was standing, rather that sitting, at that moment. The 'mind games' aspect of that moment was very beautiful for those 'in on' what was happening. That particular piece of theater had been staged at that time by the man to whom my friend had originally entrusted the key. My friend had started to worry – and that, combined with his pent-up frustration and sexual energy, clearly affected his clarity of thought. The man who had originally been trusted with key, and who had devised this (cruel) ruse, let him suffer for most of the afternoon, before – out of sight – suggesting to others that they started dropping increasingly obvious hints about where the key could be found. Realization did occur in the evening – but only after two or three more intensely anxious hours. When he did discover what had been happening (as well as the key), my friend was more cross with himself for failing to recognize and then solve the clues than about his locked predicament.

Keeping safety in mind is important, but – for those with literary or intellectual inclinations – games of 'hunt the key' based on word or mathematical puzzles can be fun too. Every minute longer than a set period for, say, solving a crossword puzzle adds a day to one's time in chastity; every minute less represents a day less. Those who are most adept can, then decide for themselves, when they want to reveal their success – and, within some scope, influence their own locking periods.

One man reported online how he and his dominant had devised a rewards system for 'good' behavior and completing his (domestic) tasks satisfactorily. They used dice. Others have used playing cards or random number generating software (widely available online free of charge). This man published their particular scoresheet on several websites. The outcomes for the first roll were that he was granted orgasm for a 1, a 2 represented a day's release from his device, a 3 earned him immediate (unpleasant) 'punishment', a 4 was a wild card, a 5 meant no release from chastity for 14 days while a 6 spared him a day off from domestic tasks that were not essential every 24 hours. The system became more complex after that, but his suggestions provide an example that others could develop or amend for their own purposes.

A long-standing friend devised another approach – involving a number of similarly minded guys provide 'rotating' keyholding or supervision for one another. To be safest, those taking part would need to guarantee to be available in case of emergencies, but the essence lies in using combination 'key safes' and passing the combinations around the group. The idea appears very exciting but reality probably renders it impractical.

HEALTH

Health, in the context of chastity, is not the same as discomfort – so the two different aspects are being considered separately here. Some aspects of health are related to pain – but, again for the purposes of this book, acute painful sensations are (by seeking refuge in the medical paradigm) more akin to potential damage that could require (surgical) intervention while slower, more chronic potential damage to the body is regarded as a matter of health.

Chafing can be regarded as an aspect of discomfort that is reasonably quickly and easily remedied – as is discussed elsewhere. However three other health matters have been identified as being linked to chastity (and the use of chastity devices.)

The first is *edema* (English English) or *edema* (US English) – in which fluid accumulates when the skin is partially damaged. While this is more generally associated with other parts of the body and other medical conditions, it has been reported by guys in chastity devices. In such circumstances, the skin is not broken externally, but internally – allowing fluid to leak from cells that have been injured into the layers of the skin. This can happen when, for example, scrotal skin gets trapped in the hinge on the back ring of some devices or part of the cock skin gets jammed. One writer online has suggested that such squeezing can occur with 'additions' to some devices, such as the Keep Sake Device (KSD) for the CB-6000. The remedy – which can be reasonably quick – is to adjust the fit.

The second potential trepidation results from the blood supply to the genitals. If circulation is poor, perhaps because an oedema is making a cockring tighter or because such rings are generally too small, then the cock and balls can feel cold and look darker. The expression *blue balls* is also sometimes used – to describe the effect on the skin of the sac, where blood vessels can be very near the surface, when the flow of blood is restricted. No lasting damage seems to occur if this only happens for short periods. This could be when a guy has a raging erection while wearing a reasonably tight cockring, but the blood should return to the sac when the erection subsides. If the discoloration lasts and the balls feel cold for more than a short time, then the safest action is to remove any constricting band around the cock and balls. Keyholders, as well as locked guys, should be aware of this possibility – and be ready to allow the removal of a device if this happens.

If the sensation of cold is very intense and the sac skin darkens significantly, then cockrings should be removed quickly. Emergency room staff have reported occasions of having to remove such devices from 'excited' men quickly, before long-term damage has been caused. However, using ice or extremely cold water to shrink an erection and allow release may avoid the embarrassment of calling for medical assistance. (This principle – of 'killing' the testes by stopping the blood flow – explains why very tight elastic bands are used as a means of castration. This is primarily, but not exclusively, in livestock such as rams, billy goats and bulls.)

Simple metal rings – made for animal harnesses – are available in a range of sizes as cockrings relatively cheaply. (Farm and tackle stores or outlets may sell them even less expensively than sex or adult retailers). Finding a size that can be worn comfortably for a reasonable length of time – probably between two weeks and a month – may be a useful way of establishing which of the cockrings that come with some chastity devices will be most practical. Doing this may test the patience, but it could prevent either longer-term exasperation or wasting money on an inappropriately sized chastity device. Alternatively, some guys say that if you can get a finger through the ring while it's in place the size is OK for making sure it stays in place while being big enough to get on and off.

Some men have also reported experiencing aching in their balls after they have been aroused for long periods without release. Medical texts are, not surprisingly, somewhat lacking in information about this phenomenon. However, the testes of many males tighten in the scrotum as ejaculation approaches – and it could be that it is this 'natural' constriction that increases the pressure on the balls to produce this sensation. Some have said that gently massaging the balls can relieve this sensation while others have reported that rubbing the perineum (the flesh between the back of the sac and the anus) can have a similar effect. The testes (balls) only produce sperm and do so from puberty until relatively late in a man's life. The use of vasectomy as contraception – the cutting of the 'vas deferens', the spermatic tube or cord – does not stop the balls from producing sperm. The vasectomy stops the sperm from getting to the prostate to become 'ejaculate'. Instead, when they have nowhere to go, the sperm are absorbed by the body. Sperm that are 'going nowhere' because a guy is in chastity are likely to be absorbed in the same way.

However, the route taken by sperm – through tubing into the body to the prostate gland – and then to join the urethra near the bladder also needs to be considered when discussing physical health and chastity – because the greatest uncertainty surrounds the prostate.

Only men have the prostate, a gland positioned in the body above the perineum and between the back of the scrotum and the rectum. The Healthy Bear – a gay general practitioner (or primary care physician) living and working in Melbourne, Australia – described the gland as being about the size of a walnut, shaped like a doughnut. It produces seminal fluid, the liquid that carries sperm most of the way from their production in the testes through the urethra in the penis to be expelled – under some pressure – during an ejaculatory orgasm. The most important question for guys into chastity that remains unanswered is whether allowing semen to stagnate in the gland increases the risk of prostate cancer. Some solace may be found in the realization that the body has a natural way of trying to avoid this – the 'nocturnal emission' or wet dream; the discharge that occurs, usually during sleep, after a period of abstinence. The prostate also has a crucial function in producing semen and adding an alkaline to it that provides protection for sperm from what the Healthy Bear calls the 'acidic environment' of the vagina. For those who haven't overcome the childhood conditioning of squeamishness around anything to do with the anus, the prostate is easy to feel – by slipping a lubricated finger past the sphincter muscle of the rectum. (Some men, when the prostate is stimulated this way, or by any other 'insertable' report a desire to urinate ….)

The 'Healthy Bear' wrote on his website that … 'very little research has been done on this topic', which considering the nature of the activity and general public (if not private) attitudes is not really surprising. He added that the 'majority of the information is anecdotal and based on medical common sense'. (To reinforce this, guys into chastity should remember that using taxes to pay for research into the causes of prostate cancer does not oblige politicians or medics to face the potential embarrassment and discomfort of having to talk much about sex or sexual behavior.) A heterosexual colleague – who was assisting a non-profit organization supporting men who have been diagnosed with prostate cancer – told me he was (perhaps not altogether unexpectedly) surprised to learn that some men could achieve orgasm by stimulation of the prostate alone.

The prostate has a crucial function in producing semen and adding an alkaline to it that provides protection for sperm from what the Healthy Bear calls the 'acidic environment' of the vagina. He has also described the gland as being about the size of a walnut, shaped like a doughnut and situated between the rectum and bladder above the perineum. For those who haven't overcome the childhood conditioning of squeamishness around anything to do with the anus, the prostate is easy to feel – by slipping a lubricated finger past the sphincter muscle of the rectum. (Some men, when the prostate is stimulated this way, or by any other 'insertable' report a desire to urinate ….)

As men get older, the prostate can become inflamed or enlarged – causing various difficulties with urination, from the repeated need to piss to difficulties in actually draining the bladder and avoiding dripping. Prostate cancer – the erratic and rapid increase in the cells of the gland – has become common in men in many parts of the world. It can be fast and aggressive – and fatal. Treatments include surgery to remove the prostate, as well as chemo- and radio-therapy.

According to the Healthy Bear's website, the gene associated with breast and ovarian cancer in women has also been linked to prostate cancer, making a knowledge of family medical history an important factor in assessing the risk and justifying regular screening and other checks for men over 40. Removing the prostate – as well as other treatments – can cause erectile dysfunction, a consequence which may be more significant for male keyholders than for those who prefer to be in chastity.

For hundreds of years, the need to maintain – and expand – the human population was such that political and economic leaders, usually in the name of organized religion, tried to promote penetrative vaginal sex, without any form of contraception, as the only expression of love, manifestation of enthusiasm or 'release' that was socially acceptable. Masturbation was stigmatized as was any form of sexual expression that was not intended to result in procreation rather than be a form of recreation. Health myths were perpetuated without challenge, despite other – greater – medical dangers. The consequence, similarly for centuries, was repeated epidemics of sexually transmitted infections – from the spread of syphilis that undermined the war effort between 1916 and 1918 or the global incidence of HIV at the end of the 20th century and start of the 21st. However, even the unchallenged power of the pulpit, a principal means of political control and sexual education before the emergence of the mass media, could not prevent such pandemics. Even in the early years of HIV education, many leading medics remained skeptical and reluctant to promote (mutual) masturbation or non-penetrative sexual activities as healthy alternatives.

Indeed, the myths were such that, by 2014, the website of the

Prostate Cancer Foundation in the United States, stated: 'High levels of sexual activity or frequent ejaculation have been rumored to increase prostate cancer risk. This is untrue. In fact, studies show that men who report more frequent ejaculations may have a lower risk of developing prostate cancer. Having a vasectomy was originally thought to increase a man's risk, but this has since been disproven.'

For many years, the most significant serious, peer-reviewed scientific research had come from the University of Sydney in Australia. However, more recent information came from a small team from the University of Quebec in Canada in 2014. A realistic overview of much of the research available was published in 2010, as a book called *Let Sleeping Dogs Lie? What men should know before being tested for prostate cancer* by Simon Chapman, Alexandra Barratt and Martin Stockler. (The Sydney University Press paperback – ISBN 978 192 089 9684 – could, in 2015, be downloaded as a pdf free of charge.)

In this, the authors 'look at very recent evidence from Australia about what men undergoing treatment for prostate cancer can expect in terms of continuing sexual function and continence'. They also state that epidemiological data from 2007, the latest they had available, challenged popular beliefs about the incidence of the disease, saying: 'What the rises mean is simply that *more* men are being tested and because of this, more cancer is being found'. (The italics are theirs.) They also challenged information released by organizations that should know better – adding that much misinformation about prostate cancer has been circulating and widely reported. Consequently, anyone can rapidly discover that accurate information is very difficult to obtain and that substantiating the claims and evidence from many studies and published papers can be even more challenging.

As far as the context of chastity is concerned, the book includes a reference to a study that was published in the *Journal of the American Medical Association (JAMA)* in 2004, which said: 'Our results suggest that ejaculation frequency is not related to increased risk of prostate cancer'. However they also point to another study – published in 2009 – which showed that men who 'engaged in frequent masturbation, of about two to seven times a week, during their 20s and 30s, had a higher rate of prostate cancer, while men who engaged in masturbation once a week during their 50s had a lower rate'.

The 2014 Quebec report, which was published in the journal *Clinical Epidemiology*, was based on studies carried out between September 2005 and August 2009, so the data was between five and nearly 10 years old by the time it became more widely available. Although one main finding – that those with 20 or more sexual partners in their lifetimes had a lower risk of developing prostate cancer than those with fewer – was publicised so successfully that this single conclusion was reported by news outlets around the world, the paper in the journal raises more questions than it answers.

The researchers considered factors such as the number of sex partners and orientation, their gender and the frequency of orgasms claimed by interviewees as well as how old they were when they first had 'intercourse' the three women who wrote the paper 'postulate that the protective effect of having had several female sexual partners may relate to a greater frequency of sexual intercourse of ejaculation.

'Although reasonable,' they added, 'this explanation remains speculative as our study did not collect information on these practices. Other measures related to sexual activity could be addressed in future investigations, include condom use, masturbation practices and the type of intercourse that occurred with each partner'.

This final sentence raises concerns – because it implies that only 'intercourse' may involve semen moving through the prostate en route to ejaculation rather than any other form of stimulation. The authors cited a single paper, published in 2002 and based on research before then, which suggested that 'physical trauma' to the prostate 'is believed to' increase levels of prostate-specific antigen. They add: 'Should receptive anal intercourse result in prostatic trauma, higher PSA levels, along with higher prostate cancer diagnosis rates, would be expected to be observed in men engaging in it.

'Potentially, the physical pounding of the prostate glad during receptive anal intercourse may itself possibly lead to a greater risk of prostate cancer; previous studies have linked the receipt of physical trauma to the breast and the testicles with breast and testicular cancers,' they said.

However, only single studies are cited to support this speculation. The authors mention only 'physical pounding' of the prostate during receptive anal intercourse but make no mention is made of less intense physical stimulation of the prostate. They did not define either 'pounding' or 'trauma' in this context and the speculation seems to imply that anal penetration can never be anything else.

The extent of the research may have been limited by how much money was available to pay for it. However, the suggestion that further questions could be asked about other practices in future research does not go as far as to indicate that these may be about stimulation or penetration other than 'intercourse' or that guidance would be sought from men's health advisers who could provide useful suggestions about the appropriate questions to ask.

However, ignoring the limits of the researchers' imaginations and the questions they ask, the rational alternative to the possibility of semen becoming stagnant in the prostate is to prevent that happening. The easiest option is to ejaculate. An alternative is to massage the prostate – gently – to provide stimulation and encourage a 'throughput' of semen while avoiding any trauma or pounding.

The wording and conclusions of the various studies suggest that none of the researchers has any appreciation of the nuances of 'brachio-proctal stimulation' – more colloquially known as 'fisting'. While some – who have been practising and practising – for significant periods of time may have sphincters that relax sufficiently for them to be 'punch fisted', others need to be penetrated more gently. Many practitioners would argue that the greatest pleasure emanates not from being violated energetically but from being opened very slowly, gently and sensuously. Similarly, the size of even a relatively small clenched fist is such that the entire prostate would be subject to pressure rather than a limited area. Also, the angle of penetration during 'intercourse', whether it is during fucking, or being opened by a dildo or some sort, determines whether the prostate is rubbed or hit. All these factors are significant and, in the great methodological tradition of assessing and then eliminating all the variables.

The medical research jury still does not appear to have been presented with adequate evidence to make recommendations one way or another, but the impression to be gleaned from such research as does exist is that some gentle stimulation of the prostate to try to event semen stagnation would not go amiss – and it can be fun too.

Warmly-welcomed research published in May 2015 that indicated that genetic mutations had been identified that could enhance the treatment of men with advanced prostate cancer is clearly encouraging, but equally such developments should not be regarded as an excuse for complacency as far as preventative measures are concerned.

In the context of other infections, being locked does, of course, reduce some risks per se, simply because penetration of others is prevented. As is mentioned elsewhere, using urethral plugs can rub and damage the internal membranes, leading to urinary tract infections if you're not careful. Other infections may nevertheless occur. Yeast infections should be treatable without having to remove a device, other than, perhaps, for avoiding embarrassment while seeing a doctor. Guys who enjoy anal penetration should never forget that the relatively thin but simultaneously highly absorbent rectal membranes are 'open doors' for many other sexually transmitted infections.

Concerns have also been raised online about a condition called *Pyronie's disease (or syndrome)* where changes to the skin of the penis may lead to changes in its appearance and 'customary curvature'. The consensus from a relatively small, non-medical, series of responses was that this was more likely to be caused by far greater physical injury than is likely to occur through chastity or as an effect of either another medical condition or, possibly even, its treatment.

LOCKS

Choosing a padlock may seem easy – but, as a tale elsewhere illustrates, that is not always true. Each needs to be selected carefully – as many models may be neither waterproof nor water resistant. Just because a brand is fiercely marketed does not guarantee its quality. Some major brands have been known to seize inside within hours and a single exposure to a shower, bathtub or swimming pool. Similarly, the most expensive may not be the most reliable either.

Numbered plastic tags are increasingly easily available, especially from online suppliers. However, the identification numbers on some can be rubbed away relatively quickly. The longevity may be extended by a covering of nail varnish, for example. Small cable ties also represent an inexpensive alternative – and these can be marked to deter removal too. Needles can be used to make patterns of holes that can then be photographed to provide evidence of any tampering. Such ties can also be far smaller than plastic tags – especially if the ends are cut off. However, if you do this, it's important to leave just enough room for the blade of a pair of scissors to be inserted for when removal is permitted while the sharp ends of cut ties should also be smoothed (with emery paper) so that the skin of the cock is not cut when, as is probably inevitable, they move round. Customised tags are available, at a price, for those who want them – and offer an alternative to engraved padlocks. Using such tags does have psychological as well as physical implications: 'Frankly,' one guy said online, 'I'd find a plastic seal humiliating. A lock is a statement about owning my manhood.'

LOCKING – or getting a device in place

Actually getting the cock into a device can be difficult, especially early on when a man is anticipating what is about to happen and excited at the prospect.

If a cage is a relatively tight fit, then getting the cock in may not be easy either. Men with foreskin may also find that getting it into a position which is comfortable is also a problem. One method that has become widely used involves using the nylon from a stocking or a pair of tights. After getting a back ring into place, a short length of 'hose', say about a foot or 30 centimeters long, is pushed through the 'piss slit' at the end of the cage and then back around the cock, with the open end of the stocking as close to the body as possible. Put the cage against the cock and then, as the nylon is pulled, the cock will be drawn in. When the cage is locked, pull out the last of the nylon.

LONG-TERM LOCKING

Who knows most about chastity, the lockee or the locker? The question is an important one – and often overlooked. Guys who like being locked frequently have a more detailed knowledge of the devices available and which is most suitable and practical for them. Those who find themselves involved as keyholders may have less experience and expertise. Locked guys can use this to their advantage – which is perhaps another reason why many like being locked by others 'on the receiving end' who may know some of the tricks used to try to elicit an early escape and can see through them very quickly. (The section covering *Keyholding* in Part I is worth [re-]reading to go with this.)

As the *Emergencies* section details, cutting the hasp of a small padlock is reasonably straightforward and most hospital emergency rooms have metal shears that will do that. Plastic tags can be cut very easily. However, breaking a device to allow release could be unnecessarily embarrassing – especially at a time of additional distress – and be extremely costly. So what do you do? The most practical approach is for the lockee to have emergency access to a key or the combination necessary to unlock a device. Either can be kept very easily in a tamper-proof way – from a small envelope made additionally secure by a signature or other mark across the seal or in some sort of breakable locket. (Having a key unreachable on a necklace can add yet another psychological dimension to the experience – because the lockee will frequently be aware of its presence yet cannot do anything about the device between his legs. Every time he thinks about the key, he is reminded of his predicament.

Quite a lot of men report being able to pull their penises out of various devices, yet far fewer seem capable of reinserting their cocks into cages or other tubes once they are out. Add-ons are – such as sharp polycarbonate points – can be attached to devices such as the CB series as a further deterrent, but once a cock is out and cannot be replaced, the 'freedom' is clearly visible to the keyholder. Evidence of when a cock had escaped may not be available, requiring honesty from a locked guy when reporting such occurrences, if the two are apart and meeting only occasionally – unless other monitoring measures are put into place.

Being permanently locked may appear ferociously erotic and simultaneously emotionally powerful and amazingly intimate. Filling the keyhole of a padlock with superglue, irrevocably damaging, for example, the head of a screw or having a device riveted into place may seem to represent total fulfillment – but the long-term implications must be considered. Just how quickly could someone be released in a medical emergency? What would happen if they faced metal detectors? Everyone may think that they are 'settled', with an established way of life, but the unforeseen can and does occur. While not wishing to deter those for whom such permanence is a life-fulfilling aspiration, remembering to put reason ahead of the libido in such circumstances cannot be emphasized enough.

LONG-TERM IMPLICATIONS

Without empirical studies, all that is available regarding the long-term implications of chastity comes from anecdotal reports, mainly posted online. As with so much, this information represents contributions from those who make the effort to offer their thoughts and experiences, while feeling sufficiently motivated (whatever the reason) to do so.

Some report that their penises appear to get smaller while others, over periods of several years, say that they – and their sexual partners – have noticed no difference, either in the size of the erect penis or the strength of any erection. Others however offer different perceptions. The size of the device and the duration of locking are other factors that need consideration. Some say that, after a couple of months or more in small cages, they may – after release – be able to masturbate and ejaculate without achieving an erection at all and that several days, and attempts at arousal, may pass before erections return to their pre-locking intensity. One man wrote online that: 'I found that after 12 months of 24/7 being locked into chastity, that my cock had permanently lost over one inch in length and width even when erect.

'When I was with my urologist about my swollen prostate,' he continued, 'I asked him about my smaller penis. He said that in order for a penis to remain capable of erections, and to maintain its full erection-size, the penis needs to be exercised daily; and that this exercise occurs either through conscious sexual arousal or else through unconscious, involuntary erections during sleep.

'He said that the penis *needs* to "inflate" several times throughout the night or it will atrophy somewhat' although this claims does seem scientifically questionable.

This man was wearing a device that was sufficiently close fitting that is prevented him from becoming erect at all. His belief was that the spongiform tissue of the 'cavernosa' in the penis 'withered' if it was not regularly inflated (as happens during an erection). He went on to report that his penis had lost about two inches of its length after about two years and that he was experiencing erectile dysfunction. Even after a period of masturbation, he only get 'semi-hard' and not achieve an orgasm, he said, and he would rub the shaft so raw in the process that he had to stop touching himself for a day or two.

The same man said that, after the two years in the device, the appearance of his cock had changed too. While the glans size remained unaltered, the thin, perpetually flaccid shaft had become too weak to support it and it 'dangled' more. The smaller shaft was, he added, an 'embarrassment because it resembles a woman's clitoris when she is sexually aroused'.

His message prompted a response from a man who said he was a doctor. He wrote: 'If you follow a male chastity program, it is necessary from time to time to unlock the device to allow the penis to be inflated with blood and oxygen. 'I am with my Master and regularly we check this together,' he added, 'locking and unlocking the device periodically so not to damage erectile tissues.'

(One dominant I know believes that erections were unnecessary in submissive men. He advocated chastity as a route to deliberate erectile dysfunction [ED] for this reason – and chose to call one of those he had locked 'edslave'.)

Men who have been locked for shorter periods than two years have reported being able to achieve erections again – but that, even with fairly frequent stimulation and masturbation, such a recovery can take a few days. One man said: 'I believe the general consensus is that you do experience minimal shrinkage, but the effects are reversed after getting sufficient time to stretch.'

Another contradicted him, saying: 'My personal experience is that extended time in a device makes no difference to the short of long-term size of a man's penis, erect or flaccid. That is my opinion based on the last 17 years with several different men.' A third suggested that 'the penis tends to change size at various times and in different situations anyway; it's part of the original design.' A fourth said he felt his cock was smaller after about nine months, during which time he could not achieve an erection but his ball sac had stretched.

As well as experiencing seminal discharges as a result of 'milking' the prostate, some guys can achieve ejaculatory orgasms even without erections. Some men have the ability – or have been trained and conditioned – to achieve erections and then ejaculate without any stimulation of the cock whatsoever. Others can reach orgasm – with or without ejaculation – during anal arousal or from the manipulation or stimulation of the balls and sac. This is why (early) negotiations between a man seeking to be locked and a keyholder should establish the more exact nature of the chastity control being exercised.

So what happens after you're locked for a while? The views of locked guys online are fascinating – and relevant. One said he had been locked for two weeks, 'but it feels a great deal longer than that. Does it ever surprise you how little time has passed in the real world as in my head; it feels like months since I was last able to get hard.' Another had been locked for 88 days. 'I have not been erect in a long time,' he said, 'and I am curious about how things are going to go. It just seems strange that my cock will be out there.' A guy whose online nickname included 'houseboy' added: 'One advantage of chastity is that it makes you much more aware of what's happening around you and it intensifies everything you do.' His days felt, he explained, fuller and longer and the experience 'especially intensifies my desire' for his keyholder and seeing that person with another man. 'However,' he continued, 'I find that my sexual frustration peaks at about day four – although the desire remains high – and after about 12 days my libido actually drops.' He then asked: 'May be the phase after day 12 is something I need to explore more.'

His assessment of the 12-day period was confirmed by another contributor. 'After about that time, I start ramping down in the frustration department,' he said, before adding: After that 'I am on the outside of my normal kink and searching more and more for harder kink. Stuff on day one I would have shunned as too much becomes barely enough….

Others report that, when they have been locked for relatively long periods, probably several months, they experience what they describe as *cyclical horniness*. During this, a day or two of frustrating desire alternates with almost total disinterest. Just as with the initial 'testosterone hump', this can affect mood and behavior, so being aware of these potential swings is important.

'LUBRICATION' and moisturisation

If anything seems consistent from the hundreds of postings to various websites, then it is that no two men are the same as far as dealing with chafing and soreness are concerned. (Lubrication here is used in that context, rather than for anal stimulation or to ease masturbation.)

The most practical advice seems to be that someone being locked for the first time should be prepared to make several trips to the pharmacy or drugstore to find the balm that works best for him.

Some guys advocate petroleum jelly – such as Vaseline – as that is absorbed relatively slowly, but its relative 'heavyness' can also mean that clings to clothing and fabrics. Others suggest similarly viscous unguents – such as zinc and castor oil cream (often recommended as a treatment for nappy or diaper rash in babies). Those who promote the benefits of vitamins and supplements point out that zinc can accelerate healing – and so feel that this is advantageous. Thinner alternatives – such as E45 or baby oils – may also be helpful. Baby 'gel', a more viscous alternative to baby oil that should be available in pharmacies and drugstores, is the moisturiser of choice for some locked guys.

(In many parts of the world, Vaseline is now sold in 'handbag-sized' cans – about 1.5 inches or 3 centimeters in diameter – as a lip balm. The size of the container also makes it exceedingly convenient for locked men, as it fits nicely into a pocket, a briefcase or backpack. The size is also well within the liquid limits for air travel too.)

The consensus from many website contributors seems to be that water-based lubricants dry out too quickly to be practical.

MENTAL HEALTH

Some suggest that preventing masturbation benefits their mental health – because they do not get anxious about wasting time while they seek stimulation. Another reason that some guys seek chastity relationships is to increase (intimate) contact with another as a counter to feelings either of loneliness or potential insecurity. They need and seek the (regular and frequent) attention of a keyholder and the physical contact that in-person locking, checking and unlocking can bring.

Some keyholders enter arrangements that include regular reporting in by the guys they are locking; if acknowledgement is part of such agreements, then the keyholders have as much of an obligation to respond as the locked guys to do report. If 'life' gets in the way, then this should be acknowledged and made clear during the negotiation of the 'dimensions of consent' – and appropriate compromises reached. Locked guys can quickly – and understandably – lose interest if they feel their efforts are going unrecognized and unappreciated. Some keyholders appear not to appreciate the need for attention. They get their excitement whenever a lock clicks into place. After that, they appear to lose interest in both the locked guy and the dynamic, abandoning lockees in a way that has been described as being 'dumped in chastity'. Such individuals relatively quickly acquire reputations – which often, but not always, precede them.

For some men – for whom thinking about sex and release has occupied a lot of their time – 're-conditioning' themselves to accept the limitations of chastity can be challenging. Ideally, this should not be so demanding that in itself it become a cause of (clinical) anxiety. However, because so many societal norms are implicitly linked with perceptions of masculinity and 'function', the difficulties may not become apparent until a guy has been locked for a while, perhaps several weeks or even possibly months. Everything linked to the evolution of medications to counter erectile dysfunction – from the amounts that pharmaceutical giants are prepared to spend on research and development reflects this; all the marketing covertly and repeatedly emphasizes the apparent primacy of the erect, ejaculatory male orgasm ... creating social pressures that may be both unwelcome and mentally unhealthy. For a man to discover that his erection isn't necessarily important per se may seriously threaten his perceptions of 'manhood' while then realizing that was, until then, an 'all-important' penis is regarded as unnecessary to the extent of being locked away may add another significant aspect to the psychological adjustments he may have to make. Passive gay men may find this transition easier, as they may have accepted many years earlier that their principal sexual organs would be their anuses and mouths. Heterosexual men with narrower horizons may have to manage greater changes in themselves.

Emotional stability

Dealing with one's emotions while in chastity is probably more of a practicality of locked life than an aspect of the underlying psychology.

However, for some, being locked can take someone further into the submissive role than they perhaps had initially intended. This may be OK for a few days, but after a few weeks, the wider implications of apparent personality changes may – as with many aspects of chastity – affect someone's working life.

While someone who is in a position of workplace authority may become more deferential over time, shorter-term implications can affect one's behavior, especially in how someone relates to their co-workers. One guy, who is locked 'from time to time' has reported that while he loves the devotion, teasing and constant horniness, this can, he said, turn into a 'bad trip', where he experiences unpleasant, destructive frustration, neglect, rejection and being short-tempered. This is not, he said

Obsessions

While seemingly rare, obsession can present problems. In 2015, one guy posted a message on the Fetlife site under the title 'orgasm denial and sleeplessness' saying: 'I am very much addicted to checking whether (his keyholder) has been in touch or posted a picture online. It's a compulsion I can do nothing about. At night, as I attempt to sleep, I check and then see pictures and the cock begs attention, making sleep difficult.'

This psychological reaction may be more extreme and more intense than simply being woken by an erection trapped inside a device in the early hours. This guy added that he found it difficult to think of anything else when he was so aroused. He would, he said, eventually get to sleep, but wake after a couple of hours to repeat the process – and rarely getting a good night's sleep.

He then said he gets pleasure from knowing that his keyholder wants this and is causing it, adding: 'This thought makes me even more aroused and the vicious, yet delicious, cycle intensifies. The more control I give up, the more I suffer, the more is taken, makes me more and more aroused'.

As with any obsession, difficulties occur when the fixation interferes with other aspects of life, especially work. This degree of intensity may run this risk and keyholders, especially those at a distance, should be aware that infatuation of this nature could become destructive. Identifying and managing such emotions is never easy, but a conscientious keyholder should try to monitor the feelings of anyone they have locked to ensure that neither the psychological nor the physical practicalities of chastity become disproportionately damaging.

MILKING

In the context of chastity, *milking* can mean two entirely different activities. One is where a man is repeatedly made to ejaculate, so that the balls are drained of sperm and the supply of seminal fluid from the prostate is also exhausted. To achieve this can be time-consuming as each ejaculation will likely take longer to achieve. For some men, it can also be physically painful, both because the cock may get sore and because each increases the strain on the body. Nevertheless, the overall effect is that the system is milked dry.

The alternative is the (gentle) stimulation of the prostate gland, usually by rubbing with a finger tip to encourage the elimination of seminal fluid. For this, the best position for the man being milked is to kneel with his upper body bent forward to lie on a flat surface. The anus is then presented for attention. Absorbent paper, a towel or another receptacle can then be placed below the penis to catch the viscous liquid. (Some dominants believe that semen and seminal fluid are always too good to be wasted, even from a man effectively rendered impotent by chastity. Some use it as a skin balm, others as to lubricate the cock during masturbatory stimulation or demand that it is licked up.) One writer suggests applying cold water or ice to the genitals to suppress any possible erection while the testosterone-laden seminal fluid is drained from the prostate with as little pleasure or emotional involvement as possible. The sensation during prostate milking can be similar to wanting to urinate, but without this happening.

NOISE

Padlocks can move about above cages, hitting the device with every step when the wearer is moving about and producing an audible 'clunk' or 'click' each time. Some guys like this, as it is yet another reminder of their predicament (and with similar psychological dynamics as the fear or joy of exposure). Yet, this can be inappropriate or attract unwanted or unnecessary attention, particularly at work or among 'innocent' friends and family. Sometimes tops like the potential of such embarrassment, but the social or professional risks may be disproportionate. This is probably yet another consent dimension to be negotiated and agreed between the locker and the lockee.

The noise can certainly be reduced, if not eliminated altogether, by holding the padlock against the cage with a strong elastic band. Alternatively, wrapping the lock in a rubber band should deaden some, if not all, of the sound.

Some suggest using (waterproof) Velcro to attach the lock to the cage while others have reported using 'rubber dots' – sold in hardware stores to prevent ornaments moving around in display cases – or other rubber or plastic coatings.

PAIN

Perceptions of 'pain' have been changing significantly during the last decades of the 20th century and the first of the 21st. Pain is now widely accepted by psychologists and physicians as being a learned response; .a signal that damage could occur if a body is not moved away from the cause of the sensation, be it the primary senses of feeling – such as temperature or impact. A simple explanation comes from the example of children and heat. However often a child may be told that putting a hand too near a flame will cause 'intense discomfort' because they will experience 'pain' and they may be 'hurt' or damaged – by burning – if they touch a hot stove, yet they probably will not actually learn that lesson until they experience the sensation The nervous system, especially within the sensations of touch and temperature, is a warning arrangement, alerting the brain to move the body away from the source of intense heat or impact so that (permanent) damage does not occur. However, the critical psychological factor is that of degree. Being warm can be pleasant; being too hot can burn and damage us. Draw the tip of a feather along the skin and the lightest of sensations can be so intense that it could easily be perceived as agony. (Close your eyes and this sensation is

very similar to that of a sharp blade being drawn along the flesh.)
This is fundamental flight-or-fight instinct that remains part of the
human state.

The historic concept of 'pain' has been challenged more frequently
in the 21st century in the BDSM context also. This may be because
learning that a particular sensation can actually be pleasurable when
it is more intense can require 'unlearning' childhood conditioning
before adjusting the threshold at which the brain engages the flight
response. (For me, caning was established during my childhood as
negative. As an adult, I encountered men for whom the activity was
positive – and sexual; they would be erect while it was happening.
One helped me overcome my childhood conditioning – by
encouraging masturbation while being beaten. I would have to count
down from ten to zero as orgasm and ejaculation approached. I was
allowed to count upwards if the intensity was too great, but it
increased steadily as four became three and two became one. The
hardest stroke of all was timed to coincide with the zero. Undoing
the negativity of my early years was achieved relatively quickly this
way.)

So, 'pain' per se is the body's way of communicating that part of
the anatomy or physiology is not functioning correctly – and that
action is needed to prevent (permanent) damage. Learning the
difference between discomfort and pain is vital for anyone who
'enjoys kink'. Keyholders and dominants similarly need to learn
enough about their submissives and their subjects to be able to
differentiate between the two – and make sure that appropriate action
is taken should a locked guy experience pain.

Similarly, a guy may react to the short-lived, but relatively intense,
pain of (for example) a ball being squeezed or forced against a chastity
device cockring while bending down. He may wince or shriek, but that
is unlikely to have caused permanent damage. The ball could be
bruised and while more serious damage is possible, it is also unlikely.
Bruising heals relatively quickly anywhere on the body. The mantra
has – for both locked guys and their keyholders – be to check and not
to take refuge in the machismo by trying to brazen it out.

Men's bodies do react differently when they are in chastity – and paying attention to the differences both physically and psychologically is important. Some Dom/sub relationships are such that the Dom requires the sub to keep a journal of his emotions and feelings about what is happening, the power that is being transferred and the control that is being exercised. Certainly in the early days of being locked – for the first few times a man is locked for more than, say, a week – he would be well advised to maintain a record of how his body and his mind are reacting.

Men – generally – have a poor reputation for being aware of their (our) own bodies and health. We seem reluctant to carry out the self-examination routines that are recommended as far as testicular cancer is concerned, for instance. A guy who is locked is well recommended to spend a few minutes each day, perhaps either in the short time before going to bed or while showering in a morning, to see how his balls feel and to check for any chafing around the groin. Such inspections can be part of regular cleaning routines but are certainly worth doing at least once a day when a guy is first becoming accustomed to being locked.

If anything out of the ordinary or suspicious is found, then the keyholder should be alerted. However important chastity may be to a man's psychology, the mental benefits and rewards should never outweigh any risk of – long-term – physical damage. Having an alternative device or the strength of mind to resist temptation without a device can be used while any minor wound heals. But, however tempting it may be for a locked guy to bleat about 'pain', damage is usually physically evident, so he should be careful about crying wolf (as the expression goes) too often.

For some, being able to endure intense sensation is a challenge – often of their conceptions of masculinity. A 'real man' should be able to 'take' a beating, for example, without complaining, or crying or complaining. Those men may also have deep conditioning that associates homosexuality with femininity – a link that they are, perhaps for reasons of self-justification or self-acceptance, trying to deal with or overcome too. They feel good when they have done so and disappointed within themselves if they have screamed or, in some way, 'shown weakness'. Others find techniques of concentration which allow them to experience the 'pain' of a beating so they can bask in the afterglow resulting from the combination of emerging bruising and an endorphin 'high'.

An additional facet to this is that 'abdicating' the decision to judge when intense sensation could cause damage requires immense trust – and this in its own right can produce truly great emotional intimacy and 'connection' between those involved. For some, this may be more powerful and significant than the physical stimulation itself.

PERMANENCE

Being locked forever may appeal, but the reality of life means that – for most people – this is likely to remain within the realm of fantasy rather than everyday living.

Some factors that militate against permanence are entirely practicalities, identified and discussed elsewhere in this book. They include, for example, constraints of work, travel and being around friends and family. However, like so much, the length of locking will vary according to individual circumstances – and each is different. So, again, rules do not exist and the only people who can establish any parameters are the locker and the lockee, having (once again) gone through the negotiation of each dimension of consent to agree a regime that is exciting, erotic and feasible. Probably the greatest criterion to use in assessing each factor is common sense.

Attitudes towards the psychological implications of permanence vary too. One online questioner said he felt that a man's orgasm was like a 'safety valve in a pressure cooker', in that every male needs to 'let off steam' every so often to prevent explosions of insanity. Chastity can block the valve, he suggested, so an alternative outlet is necessary. 'I feel that being locked … permanently, without this, is expecting too much. I suspect many dominants do not have any real understanding of (male) sexuality or how to manage it properly.' Totality was too much for this guy and, he said, a deal breaker.

The responses included the recognition that any power

relationship has to be two-way, regardless of metabolic aspects such as prostate care. Another suggested that some dominant women give the impression of having no idea of this aspect of the male psyche, thinking that they can exploit the situation to get something for nothing.

Another contributor to the discussion differentiated between permanence and being ignored. The psychology of consensual cuckolding is not covered in this book, as the underlying belief here is that chastity can be a way to enhance interaction between two people, and increase the intimacy between them, rather than taking improper advantage of unrequited dedication. A further respondent said that a woman he had met considered that her keyholding alone was providing him with a free service and that if he needed anything else, it was 'topping from the bottom'. The guy who raised this particular aspect of the dynamic went on to say that, for him, the mental side of this would be 'horrendous'. One of the biggest attractions of chastity, he suggested, was the 'possibility' of release.

'The male body,' he wrote, 'is magical. I have been in chastity exactly 100 days with no removal and no issues. Now, just being able to bring my (keyholder) to orgasm each week orally, my body will weep fluids. I have come very close to orgasm a few times, just doing this and with no penile stimulation.

'However,' he added, 'if you just shut down completely, what's the purpose of a device? Yes, men of different cultures will go with any orgasm for life/years because of their religious beliefs ... but I need attention and I want to give sexual attention. If I was locked away with no sexual contact, it would not work for me.'

Confirmation of the difference between permanent chastity and the lack of intimacy came in the final contribution to this exchange. This guy said he could imagine a relationship with someone who demanded permanent orgasm denial as being very fulfilling – as long as they shared romance and sex. A lack of interest from a keyholder can render chastity no more than cold, impersonal and boring.

PREMATURE EJACULATION

Men who experience premature ejaculation have also reported that chastity has helped bring greater fulfillment to their relationships. One guy, for example, identified this particular physiological aspect of locking by saying: 'I've long since come to terms with the fact that I don't "last" very long and that it takes me hours to recharge for another round.' Consequently, he explained, he liked being locked so he could focus his attention on his partner – and knowing he wasn't going to be released helped him 'free his mind' to devoting himself to that. 'Such times are the most satisfying,' he said, even though the partner wasn't keen on keeping him permanently locked. He did add that he loved orgasms, alternating between wanting more or none. If within the power dynamic, he was never allowed another orgasm, he would, he said, be happy – as it was all about the dynamic not just the chastity,

PUNISHMENT

Punishment is also a topic that needs consideration in this context. In some cultures, the word 'punishment' has become synonymous with aspects of BDSM, especially relating to what can otherwise be called 'impact' or 'percussion' play; in other words, hitting someone. The expression CP – corporal punishment – can be seen as institutionalizing the concept, because the idea of caning, spanking or beating someone to inflict pain was, for generations, regarded as an acceptable motivating factor in education or the military. The most logical explanation of how such activities, especially for the person seeking such stimulation, come within the BDSM or kink remit comes from the psychologist Erik Berne, in his seminal work *Games People Play*. Berne's hypothesis suggests that the only way some children can attract the attention they so desire from parents is by being naughty – and, because the parent then inflicts 'punishment' of some sort, the sensation and attention are very strongly linked as part of the 'conditioning' of the 'formative years'. Some therapists therefore regard 'punishment' in any form as 'negative reinforcement' and mentally unhealthy.

If 'punishment' is agreed within the negotiation of the dimensions of consent, then the activity that will be require in the event of 'failure' genuinely has to be one which the submissive does not like. One dominant I encountered during my formative years in SM believed that beating of any form was far too good to be used as a punishment. Intense stimulation in that form was to be employed positively, as a reward, with the recipient being encouraged to enjoy the delights of an endorphin high while simultaneously pleasing (and sexually exciting) the dom.

Such activities should, therefore, probably include discomfort (but not pain per se, physical or psychological damage). They may involve deprivation – of attention or stimulation – or other restrictions. For many, in the 21st century, with so much going on throughout their waking hours, the withdrawal of means of communication can be a serious challenge. Boredom frightens many of us. Being sent to the 'naughty step' to think about what we have done, or being consigned to 'our rooms' without access to any form of entertainment or other stimulation allows little alternative but to consider our predicament. Some, especially those raised within some religious cultures, can 'do guilt' extremely effectively without any further, external, reinforcement. The inner trauma fuelled by feelings of having let down someone important can be so great that further measures are little more than symbolic. That said, they are however still probably worthwhile – if only as means of maintaining the dynamic and roles within a power relationship.

RECREATIONAL MEDICATIONS

While the 'inappropriate' use of medications should probably not be encouraged, such behavior happens. When it does, it's also equally probably that it should be done as safely as possible and with as much knowledge and information as possible.

For some who are locked, the frustration can be increased – if not enhanced – by medications licensed for the 'treatment' of erectile dysfunction such as Viagra and Cialis. Clearly using such (intense) pharmaceutical products should really only be used after being prescribed (by an appropriately qualified physician).

However, trying to deny that such 'recreational' use of such medications does happen would be unwise. Keeping a locked or controlled guy in a state of added arousal can be great fun, for the top and, through the increased frustration, the bottom too.

If these are acquired illicitly, by buying online or elsewhere, establishing whether the medications are genuine may be a first consideration; the quality may be a second. If you use the 'real' product, then reading the detailed instructions – and 'contra-indications' information, either online or if a printed leaflet is supplied – is essential. The manufacturers warn, for example, that other 'enhancements' such vaso-dilators, best known as 'poppers', should never be used by anyone at the same time as Viagra; the effect on the heart could be very serious indeed, if not fatal.

Testosterone (replacement) therapy may also appeal to those into chastity play. The most readily available versions of this are sprays or gels that can be applied to the skin – and absorbed into the body that way. The effectiveness of this process greatly as the ability of the body to absorb anything varies according to the thickness of the skin and the number of nearby blood vessels. The instructions for these often suggest that they are applied to places such as the inside of the wrist – where the pulse can be so easily felt – often after a hot shower or bath as these boost the blood flow and circulation.

Some men report feeling horny very soon after applying such gels or sprays while others report anecdotally that repeated prescribed use has the effect of generally increase and otherwise non-existent libido. The faster reaction may be due more to psychological hopes and expectations than the metabolism, but could be exploited to try to increase frustration for a locked guy.

For men whose testosterone levels are exceedingly low, some physicians prescribe 'shots'. Injectable testosterone – especially the genuine product – may be far more difficult to acquire illicitly. While needle exchanges in many places have reduced infection risks from sharing equipment, having confidence in the quality of the product, being able to measure dosages and inject safely add significant dangers to this practice.

RELATIONSHIPS

If locker and lockee find one another because of a mutual interest in chastity, then communication between them is probably easier than if one person has, or develops, the fascination later. This is especially pertinent in situations where one develops or discovers (submissive) tendencies towards the other which had not previously been identified or explored.

Talking about sex in many cultures or between generations is frequently difficult. Written, especially electronic, communication can reduce potential embarrassment and be easier than talking. Desire is inseparable from the risk of rejection; therefore communicating about any aspect of longing can be difficult.

Therefore, if one partner wants something, the skill lies in being able to ask the other without either the topic or the question being in the least uncomfortable. Where a desire may appear 'unusual' or beyond social norms this may appear additionally difficult. Where there has been, or may even still be, repression of some sort, either individual or societal, sexual communication can be even more complex and delicate.

The predicament can be particularly acute if one of those in a relationship wants to introduce a new or 'different' activity, such as 'kink' of some sort into what would otherwise be considered 'vanilla' interaction. When one man raised such a question online, the respondents offered a variety of suggestions. One emphasized that 'communication is the key' (without appreciating the pun). 'Make sure,' he said, 'you both talk things through at each step, so you remain on the same page. The goal, he continued, is to make your partner feel comfortable. If they are hesitant to make decisions for you, then be patient. 'Lock yourself because *you* want to see how it feels,' he suggested, and then explain how much fun it is to be teased while being unable to do anything about it. 'Explain how you didn't realize how much looking at the partner turned you on until the cage made it ... harder to express,' he added. Your intention is to help the partner enjoy that experience too and want to repeat it. Try not to behave differently and express gratitude for the interest and provide reassurance that the partner is reacting the way you had hoped, and encourage that as positively as you can. (Yes this can be regarded as being similar to the 'upwards management' – if not manipulation – skillfully wielded by a pushy bottom, but once the partner gains confidence and learns more about you, that *should* change.

Counsellor, therapist and author Andrew G Marshall has specialised in relationship communication – and has written in great detail about the difficulties that have been first encountered and then overcome. In his 2012 book *Make Love Like a Prairie Vole; Six Steps to Passionate, Plentiful and Monogamous Sex*, he includes 'unlocking your fantasies' as step five. He suggests that fantasies exist on two levels – those we comfortably reveal, which are 'respectable' and actually say little about us. We only disclose second level fantasies very reluctantly. They are, he says, detailed and sometimes disturbing. He also uses the word 'dirty'.

The crux is the way we each relate to 'normality' or social convention and the attitudes and beliefs that surrounded us during our 'formative years'. What is 'dirty' or even 'disturbing' to one person may be rationalised, entirely understandable, logical and as far from censure or reproach as it is possible to be, while someone else is appalled and outraged by the existence of such concepts, let alone such realities. Attitudes change over time too – so age differences as well as the background of each partner probably need to be talked about first, so each has a better idea of 'where the other is coming from'.

Mr Marshall cites the five most popular fantasies identified by researcher Professor Brett Kahr and published in 2007. These include being dominant or assertive (33 per cent), being passive or submissive (29 per cent), bondage – active or passive – 48 per cent and blindfolding someone, 17 per cent.

Such maturity may be encouraging, but many dictionaries still define 'kink' as something strange or wrong. The terms are negative, reflecting the values or beliefs of the compilers or the publishers at the time when the work was carried out, often well before publication. In sexual terms, kink may be regarded as the unconventional – but the key derivative word is, even if it has yet to appear in dictionaries, 'kinkster' – to denote those who transpose their fantasies into reality.

Clearly, where the control of one individual by another is concerned, clear dangers are involved. These may be psychological or physical – and the potential for abuse is ever-present. For the kinkster, the obligation is to ensure that the manifestation of their activity is healthy and that the individual being and human rights of each are respected.

In societal climates where equality is perceived as paramount, acknowledging – let alone challenging – this by introducing the concept of 'power dynamics' can be discomforting to the extent of being threatening. When women's rights are so abused in many societies and even in 'developed' western cultures, the move from women being 'chattels', expected to 'honor and obey' their dominant, masculine husbands is perceived as being a relatively recent social change.

Additionally, gender roles and perceptions which have been adopted, often subconsciously by copying and mimicry, during childhood probably lie at the core of much discomfort in talking about sex in general and specific turn-ons in particular.

Being open and honest about one's desire and need to transform a fantasy into a reality also involves great trust – potentially more than is assumed in many relationships. This challenges mutual psychology – the fear of rejection and that someone you love will 'think less of you' (whatever that means) because you have such fantasies and want to explore them.

Exploring intensity – be it physical or psychological – does require great faith and confidence, be that in a kinky one-night-stand or within a longer, monogamous relationship. Simply being scared of how a partner may react can be destructive in itself – and deny one, perhaps even both, partners great fulfillment.

So, how do you breach the subject with a partner? Andrew Marshall identifies points to keep the discussion 'positive and productive'. He starts by advising that the person wanting to explore a fantasy first has a clear idea of what their fantasies are about and what they are trying to achieve. For those accustomed to the weekly, perhaps monthly, impersonal penetration, in the missionary position, in bed, in the dark, without much intimacy or foreplay, between partners who have never seen each other naked or explored their bodies, this alone can be a test.

Mr Marshall's next suggestion is strategy he calls 'appreciative inquiry'. He suggests telling a partner about what is most pleasurable in their existing sexual activity. The technique starts by celebrating the successful and enjoyable and then seeking to extend that. (Mutual sexual gratification seems impossible without feedback. Sometimes someone may feel embarrassed about expressing pleasure, perhaps experiencing guilt that they are getting more out of what is happening than their partner, whom they feel should take priority. In power dynamic settings, the dominant may challenge the submissive to be silent.)

Breaching the subject may be easiest and least threatening after good sex. Sharing the thought that 'that was good' may then be steered from an agreed 'yes it was' towards, as Andrew Marshall suggests, 'well, how can we make it even better?' (He also here recognizes that perceptions of what constitutes 'sex' also vary. In some parts of the world, anything that isn't vaginal penetration is not 'proper sex' and that everything else is foreplay. An activity may be 'sexy', but is it 'sex'? For some men, raised in cultures where heterosexual machismo is prime, mutual masturbation with another guy, or even sucking, is not 'sex' and, therefore, they do not consider themselves to be bisexual, let alone homosexual. In some all-male settings, the shared experience – 'where needs must' – become a socially acceptable rationale and justification for appreciating and enjoying the realization that being masturbated by another hand can be nicer than one's own.)

Popular mythology has much to answer for. Somehow we learn to believe that genitals should only be stimulated very gently, that 'intensity' is the same as 'pain', but neither is true. So, just as a partner can be encouraged to stimulate particular body parts, by the suggestion that pulling, stroking, licking or sucking a little harder would be better, so the concept of chastity can be introduced in a similarly roundabout and unthreatening way. The suggestion that 'wouldn't it be better if I saved it for you?' may be one approach, or 'wouldn't it be good if you came first?' could come from the more passive partner, so that the focus of the sex, or lovemaking, is subtly shifted. It could be the opposite: 'Wouldn't it be better if I came first?' or 'Wouldn't it be better if you really did save it for me – and not masturbate between now and when we have sex again?' Alternatively, the dominant could suggest that 'I know you like to wank, but I'd really love it if you saved up all your horniness for me'.

The chances that you will both identify the same fantasies and the same wish that they should become real are very small indeed, so looking for commonalities and compromise is important. (Some, for example, may be against beating a partner, because they have no wish to 'hurt' someone they love.) However, introducing chastity within the context of 'saving and sharing' may be easier.

Once (sexual) communication has become a little less uncomfortable, the possibilities for exploration and consequent (mutual) fulfillment expand immeasurably. One technique to allow that to accelerate harmoniously is to try to identify and eliminate areas of potential misunderstanding. Andrew G Marshall says that a constant theme of his book is the need for couples to talk more – and to discuss what, for each, 'promotes and hinders' good sex. Key to that, he suggests is identifying our perceptions of gender, gender roles and gender stereotypes.

Is chastity kinky? Well, yes and no. It can involve overt power play or uncomplicated mutual adoration. It does involve the three crucial factors surrounding kink – that whatever happens is safe, sane and consensual. (Consent, it must be remembered, has its own dimensions and is far more than simply saying 'yes'. It has to be defined – and then agreed – in terms of who, what, when, where, how and even why.) Safety too should be considered both psychologically and physically.

Coming to terms with one's own psyche and desires may require consideration – and having the inner strength to reject – some societal conventions. Is it, for example, 'humiliating' to kiss another person's feet or a positive manifestation of confidence in showing affection in an 'unorthodox' way? Whose beliefs are being reflected in such words? Popular tabloid newspapers may, in news columns, be censorious about some sexual activities while small advertisements, a few pages later, may be promoting chatlines aimed at those with the self-same proclivities.

In the last of his six steps to 'passionate, plentiful and monogamous sex', Andrew Marshall identifies specific issues that can cause anxieties and difficulties – ranging from apparently incompatible libidos, misplaced gender assumptions about desire and performance (including erectile dysfunction and premature or retarded ejaculation), penis size and vaginal or anal cleanliness.

Perhaps most importantly of all, Mr Marshall offers a way for each of us to assess whether what we do or what we desire is healthy. He suggests that we should ask whether the activity increases self-esteem, whether any consequences are negative or destructive, will anyone be hurt or how will perceptions of another, loved, one be affected?

Counsellors and relationship therapists can definitely help – because they are permitted by couples to ask questions that an individual may find difficult. Mr Marshall concludes by offering a communication game – where partners take turns to ask questions. These range from asking about romance, the difference between sex and making love, embarrassment – with the human body or human communication, what constitutes foreplay, frequency, fantasy, role play and location.

Accepting chastity as part of a relationship – and becoming sufficiently confident that it becomes an overt part of the interaction, where teasing and flirting can (between the partners) no longer be restricted to the home or even the bedroom – can significantly enhance the bond between partners. What may start as a very tentative hint could be the start of increased excitement that is genuinely amazing.

Every personal experience is different. One man has told online how he and his partner had talked about chastity – 'I can't remember who initiated it,' he said – but we were both keen. A first attempt with one design was abandoned after difficulties with comfort and cleanliness but a second go, with a silicone device proved more successful. The locked guy said that he had tested the ring sizes for a few days before giving his partner the keys as a surprise. He reported being allowed out once a week for cleaning and shaving during which times he was otherwise not permitted to touch himself. 'Eventually,' he said, ' I confessed I was more felt much more comfortable with the cage on than off and being free was more like a punishment than a reward.' He added that he felt strange about adjusting to this and how it had become part of his life. 'It is a constant reminder of our love and bond and of my submission and (my partner's) dominance over me.'

Chastity can assist long distance relationships too – emotionally bringing partners together through regular checking and helping to keep the mutual focus between dominant and submissive.

REPAIRS

Some polycarbonate devices do break. The material can become brittle over time – and the designs do, by their very nature, include weak points. Some users have tried, not altogether successfully, to make repairs using superglue while others, more successfully, have used the plastic cement available (in many pharmacies or beauty outlets) for attaching artificial fingernails. Many adhesives can cause allergic reactions, from the mildly irritating to the very severe, so testing one's sensitivity with a little on, say, a piece of tape on an area of less sensitive skin than the genitals is probably advisable.

Again on Fetlife, one contributor reported that a device that had split had been repaired with 'resin impregnated carbon fibre strands', which 'stopped any sort of splitting'. However, he added: 'My keyholder never found the look very appealing though.' This technique may have been effective but clearly had an esoteric downside. The same contributor went on to say that he had repaired a 'base' ring from carbon fibre and resin – but that he never really liked the feel of the result. It was, he said, more restrictive and the angle added pressure to the ballsac.

Few chastity enthusiasts probably have sufficient grasp of materials science, the knowledge of where to purchase carbon fibre strands or the technical skills to be able to combine them with resin for this to be a widely practical approach to making one's own repairs to damaged devices.

I have known a CB2000 – based on a design using rods and bars – breaking (admittedly after falling off a bicycle – and fortunately on to relatively soft grass rather than a harder surface such as concrete). During the fall, the pressure from the spacer bars was sufficient for the sharp edges of the hole to cut a plastic security tag ... and effectively, and unexpectedly, allow escape from the device.

RITUAL

Some power relationships in which chastity is a factor use the incentives of particular occasions as opportunities for release. One man reported that for him, these included Valentine's Day, a birthday or other (religious) holidays. He also said he was sometimes only allowed out when the 13th day of the month fell on a Friday. Another reported that he was allowed an orgasm on Valentine's Day, but then had to wait four months until his birthday for another possible release. His partner, he said, wanted him to go an entire year, but this would be reviewed on his birthday and their anniversary. If the partner thought he was handing it well, restriction would continue. 'This year,' he said, 'has only two dates for possible orgasm, but quite frankly after two years of this I do not really want an orgasm. It is 10 seconds of pleasure followed by depression, sadness and "being bitchy". Then I have to eat my cum and lock immediately. I hate having to start again as the first month is hardest, although it gets easier after that.'

Another reported that, after Valentine's Day, he was told 'we'll start with a month' – but he had no idea how long he would be locked after that. He too admitted that freedom felt weird after two years of locking.

RUINED and EVENTUAL ORGASMS

The orgasm is – for most of humanity probably – the implicit and explicit climax of sexual activity. For most men, that is synonymous with what represents the ultimate pleasure that accompanies ejaculation.

However one aspect of chastity 'play' can be that the locked – and usually more submissive – partner is denied even that particular pleasure. Although ejaculation is allowed, or perhaps even encouraged, the intention is that this should not be accompanied by genuine gratification. The writer of the 'tease and denial' contribution on Wikipedia, for example, considers this to be where the genitals are stimulated to the point where orgasm would 'normally be inevitable'. Then, the writer suggests, direct stimulation is stopped or reduced to keep 'the recipient' on the very brink or *edge* (their emphasis) of orgasm but without it being guaranteed or inevitable. If, the writer continues, orgasm still occurs; it usually brings less pleasure than usually and is considered a 'ruined orgasm' (rather than a 'denied orgasm').

Orgasms, for most men, are probably 'best' ruined by providing stimulation until semen (or ejaculate) can be seen or felt where the urethra gets near to the penis, either behind the ball sac or just in front of it. (Many men also find that their balls 'tighten' towards the body when they get close to orgasm.) At that point, the stimulation stops, so the body – rather than the mind – proceeds to the release.

For some, the impact of this can be increased by powerlessness. If they are in bondage or constrained in other ways, the intensity may be increased because they cannot do anything to assist the ejaculation. Bound hands may move in a way similar to masturbation, but well away from the penis.

Another way to ruin a man's orgasm is to introduce different stimuli, ones that are so powerful that they cause a momentary distraction from the climax. For the keyholder or top, the easiest way to do this is using a sensation that would otherwise be considered painful, but which should not cause (lasting) damage. This could be, for example, dropping hot wax onto the head of the penis – from a distance where the temperature is enough to cause a significant reaction but not so great that the glans is burned – or by applying a stroke of a cane to the buttocks, or using a (clean) but sharp point to another sensitive area of the body.

Some dominants allow lockees to orgasm in a way that is more fulfilling – but only if they meet certain criteria or reach ejaculation within certain parameters.

For some, orgasm can be a reward. Some tops use this as a fitness incentive – allowing their submissives to cum if they reach, or stay within certain fitness targets, for example.

Others make the challenge more demanding. For instance, one submissive has reported that he is allowed to ejaculate if he successfully obeys strict instructions – such as reaching orgasm within an unrealistically short period of time or using a sex toy while in bondage. Failure results in punishment and being locked again without release.

Some men use being locked as self-discipline and a means of avoiding the temptation of pornography and masturbation. Others deliberately excite themselves while some are instructed to be aroused by dominant partners, even being monitored online as they do so.

Technology has made some teasing play easier. Random number generating software can be downloaded free of charge while, as has been discussed elsewhere, playing cards and dice offer more old-fashioned alternatives. Each partner could, for example, put suggestions into a mix that neither knows about – so that both can be surprised by the outcome. A dominant may instruct a submissive to write down, say, 10 or a dozen ideas, from which only six cards are chosen, either deliberately, because the dominant actively assesses each, or by chance. For the geek kinkster, compiling spreadsheets of the outcomes may provide additional pleasure.

SECURITY SCANNERS

Clearly those who travel will more frequently encounter metal detectors and body scanners at airports. However, during the early years of the 21st century, such machines were increasingly installed at government buildings in many jurisdictions. In the UK, for example, those entering courts, premises used by the (outsourced) passport office as well as the Palace of Westminster and jails must walk through such scanners. In all these locations, passing through a scanner may be followed by frisking.

While some Doms may be entertained by the thought of a submissive or a locked guy experiencing the embarrassment of more intimate scrutiny, perhaps even strip searching, however authorities' attitudes towards 'unnecessary' additional work of this sort are unlikely to be positive while those employed by some of the contractors engaged to run such services may well be paid as little as possible and not be sufficiently well-educated or broad-minded to appreciate the nuances of chastity. While silicone and polycarbonate devices may not in themselves be discovered by metal detectors, padlocks could be. Even if these materials themselves do not become 'visible' to the full body scanner machines, the impracticalities suggest that trying to go through such processes while locked is inadvisable.

Technology can, however, be used to great effect to ensure that the 'lockee' is free for as short a time as possible. However, some trust is still required, after checking in or dropping bags at an airport, a guy who is locked can be instructed to go to the men's room – and send a cell phone image to the keyholder of the device in place. The metadata for the image file will record the time at which the photograph was taken. Global positioning and similar apps may also provide proof where this happened. After that, the device should be removed and placed in a carry-on bag before going through security. Chastity devices may arouse the curiosity of security operatives but are not banned items. As soon as possible after that, the 'lockee' should return to the men's room and replace the device. A further photograph can be sent to indicate obedience, after which the key can be placed in an envelope, which is then sealed. Either put a signature or similar scrawled mark across the seal and send a photograph of that to the keyholder too. Photographs of the sealed envelope can then be sent to the keyholder at set intervals. Instant messaging apps can be cheaper than using e-mail or SMS/text messages if phone company roaming charges are expensive. (Pictures taken while a smart phone is in 'flight mode' should also include the origination time in the metadata, so a keyholder can be reasonably assured of compliance.)

SEX (WHILE LOCKED)

Being locked should not automatically be thought of as not 'having sex'. That may be true for some, but for others chastity appeals because it enhances the sexual experience and 'makes sex better'.

This may, for some, be intellectually or culturally challenging – because it obliges us to reconsider what we actually mean by 'sex'. For most of the human race, sex is goal-oriented; that goal being the ejaculatory male orgasm during penetration.

Clearly this may still be the intention for the top, but not the lockee, so the lockee's energies and enthusiasms can be put to good use by the locker.

Being locked can greatly enhance sex – because you are obliged to ignore the penis which is, for so many and so often, the entire focus of sexual activity.

A locked guy can, of course, be used as little more than a sex toy, so that the top can, if he wishes, merely use the guy as a 'fuck hole' for quick relief, be that from masturbation, fellatio or anal penetration.

Locked sex can also have great benefits for those who are in the least anxious about their performance. Those who may fret about premature ejaculation or erectile dysfunction (as bottoms) can shed such tensions because they need not worry about either cumming or being hard. Tops who feel that they can cum too quickly can relish the prospect of being able to cum at least twice – secure in the knowledge that the sex won't have to end when the partner reaches orgasm or ejaculates, because that is not going to happen. A top who does reach orgasm quickly can do so, relax while enjoying other ministrations from the locked submissive before becoming aroused in anticipation of a second, or more, ejaculations and orgasms.

If the top is concerned about his erections, he can direct the submissive to please other parts of his body – through, for example, erotic massage as well as the use of the fingers and mouth on any erogenous zone he may wish.

As with so much, the only limits are those of the imagination – and safety, so the 'dimensions of consent' should apply.

Dealing with language may well be the first obstacle that needs to be cleared in this context. Some consider SM 'play' to be sex, others do not. Clearly, those who enjoy 'body play' – which may be a more accurate and contemporary phrase to encompass more intense physical or psychological stimulation and extending the physicality from the immediate erogenous zones, such as the genitals, anus and nipples.

Some enjoy and seek body (or SM) play because they relish the endorphin high that they experience. This has been described as more of a 'drug trip' than sex, but with the natural hormone that affects the brain being produced as a result of physical stimulation rather than taking on a substance of some sort. Some get great pleasure by, for example, beating another person; this may cause arousal that becomes manifest as an erection or it may not. The excitement may come from the (negative) screaming of the bottom experiencing 'pain' or the (positive) singing of a bottom enjoying exactly the same stimulation but processing the neural signals as pleasure.

The skin is the biggest organ of the body – and while the sensitivity varies greatly between areas where there are more nerve endings or fewer – sexual arousal need not by any means be limited to the penis. In terms of body play, those involved should decide for themselves what they want … and whether that does, or does not, involve the penis or other parts of the body that are constrained.

Alternatively, the activity may be far more gentle and sensuous – although the lightest of touches (such as stroking sensitive nipples or the head of a cock through the bars of a device as gently as possible) with the tip of a feather can produce a feeling of such intensity that deciding whether it is ecstasy or agony becomes almost impossible. Simply enjoying the contact of naked skin with naked skin can be very beautiful.

This may, for example, be enhanced by relatively simple bondage – so that sensations have to be created by arts of the body other than the inevitable fingertips. For most people, vision is the dominant sense – so restricting this so the brain has no alternative but to concentrate on incoming information from the other senses can develop and boost body awareness. If you can't see, you can't worry about how someone else appears – so visual turn-ons become less important.

Probably the best advice is to allow plenty of time – and try to avoid as many possible interruptions as possible. Those who are enjoying chastity play have probably achieved sufficient intimacy and candor in communication to allow ideas for such play times, sessions or sex to be discussed. Those involved can decide for themselves about the methods of communication and, indeed, about what they want to do. That it should be pleasurable and fun – even if the gratification and such perceptions may be delayed – is vital, but within that, the scope is nearly limitless.

Simplicity can be both challenging and fun. Both top and bottom can, for example, be involved, regardless of role. Take turns, to stand or lie, either with the eyes closed or blindfold, hands to the side or bound, and let the other stimulate any part of the exposed flesh for, say, five or ten minutes at a time. This could be very sensuous or generate the exasperation of tickling; it may be arousing or relaxing. Take turns – but, after however long, all that may not be permitted is an ejaculatory orgasm or penile contact for the submissive.

So, probably the best and most practical suggestions and reminders are 'communicate' and 'explore'. With those, 'chastity sex' really could become 'better sex', even if it is – in wider social terms, at least for one person – slightly 'different sex'.

SHAVING and smoothness

Pubic hair can, very easily, become trapped in some cage devices. Perspiration can also cling to hair so having pubes, especially if the hair is longer, can increase frustrations and difficulties regarding personal hygiene for those who are locked.

Some advocate shaving – but the return of stubble and the potential for razor rash, where the hair growth is erratic and irritating may add rather than reduce discomfort. Those who are committed to hair removal may choose more permanent arrangements – such as laser treatment to destroy the hair follicles and prevent all future growth. Depilatory creams should be used very carefully around the male genitals – as the astringent chemicals used can damage relatively sensitive skin and membranes. Brands intended 'for men' have usually been formulated to deal with tougher hair on the stronger skin of the legs, arms and torso rather than for the more delicate 'bikini line' area.

If a single hair becomes trapped, it can very quickly become irrationally and disproportionately painful. For many guys, trimming – to about a quarter inch or 2-3 millimeters – is probably most practical. It can be done – carefully – with electrical trimmers and tidied with small, sharp scissors. Regular application of some balms can also, over time, cause the stubble to become softer.

For those into intense control, it has been known for a dominant to require the submissive to remove each pubic hair, individually, plucked with tweezers. Seeing this happen once, the process was slow – and represented a severe punishment. The guy was, unsurprisingly, quite sore when he finished, although this seemed worse on the pubic area than on his penis or scrotum. Calamine lotion – or a similar 'anti-itch' liquid, available in some US pharmacies and drugstores as an external analgesic – is thought to prevent or lessen the effects of razor rash and/or discomfort after plucking. Although the hair did grow back, it took several weeks before it became noticeable again. For those who are dedicated, or perhaps even directed, to manage their appearance this way, hair in such areas can be controlled by plucking again as soon as enough has appeared to be gripped by tweezers.

Some writers about SM and power play have suggested that the removal of hair can be symbolic of the taking away of manhood; this could reflect aspects of the power dynamics explored in the biblical tale of Samson or as a return to youth or even childhood. In terms of chastity, getting rid of hair around the cock and balls is probably more a matter of practicality than anything else; the extent to which other hair is removed, by what means and how frequently, are other dimensions that can be added to or explored within the dynamics of a 'power' relationship.

Keyholders can supervise shaving, either in person or 'on cam' when a sub is unlocked or involve a third person. Whichever device is most effective and causes least discomfort is probably best determined though trial and error, going through the range of razors, waxing, creams, tweezers or other plucking devices.

One keyholder reported that he insisted on his locked subs being shaved for aesthetic reasons. Firstly, he feels that some smaller devices could become almost invisible within a bush of pubic hair and secondly, he believes the contrast between the texture (and possibly color) of a device and the flesh can enhance the visual effect and the psychological. This, he suggests, can be further emphasized if the locked guy gets the opportunity to see himself in a mirror or a photograph.

SLEEP

Probably the most frustrating aspect of being locked, at least at first, is trying to sleep with a device in place. For some guys, even the weight of a relatively light device – such as a polycarbonate CB2000 or a silicone Birdlocked design with plastic tags – can be enough to pull the genitals about in ways that feel unfamiliar and uncomfortable.

Aarkey, for example, advises against trying to sleep face down, as any device will press into the groin. He recommends trying to sleep lying on your back or on your side. Some guys lie against pillows as these can provide some support for their devices, except this isn't very practical if you move around a lot.

Many men experience erections while they are asleep as a matter of course and never notice them. However, getting hard in many designs of device can be uncomfortable enough to wake someone. Even while unconscious, a device may actually stimulate the genitals enough to make erections more likely, at least initially.

For guys who like to masturbate or have sex so that post-orgasmic relaxation helps them sleep, being aroused – and aware of it – may make getting to sleep more difficult.

Also, an erection during slumber can be a symptom of a need to piss, so trying to avoid drinking too much too soon before trying to sleep is advisable. Dehydration is never sensible, so thinking about what you drink and when becomes more important – so that your body has enough water to fuel the metabolism during sleep but not so much that you're always wanting to get up to piss, regardless of whether you are locked or not.

Probably the most important single factor to remember is that you're adding potential stimulation to a sensitive area of the body that has, over many years, become conditioned to (relative) freedom. As is so often the case, time is a great healer – and being impatient is likely to extend the process of reconditioning.

If you normally sleep naked, then think about starting this reconditioning process before you are locked for the first time. Try wearing underwear to bed, especially something that is tight enough to constrain the genitals. One guy has suggested a cup jock – with the 'protector' in a pouch – as an introduction as it can create some discomfort without the distraction of an erection fighting hard against a cage.

Some guys have reported that they got used to being locked within a few days while others have said it has taken them several months. Self locking, if only at night for a few weeks, can be helpful preparation for a commitment to another – as a device can be taken off (for a few minutes) to relieve a painful 'piss hard-on' in the middle of the night, but it should be replaced immediately, perhaps with a little lube or other moisturizer.

SOLO CONSTRAINT

Some guys who do not have keyholders enjoy locking themselves – but then wonder what to do, either to make sure they remain locked or to increase their horniness.

One – who clearly had nothing better do to – would lock himself and then deny himself release until he had reached a set score playing solitaire on his computer. Another thought about dropping his key into stinging nettles while a third had frozen his in a (US) quart – about a litre – of ice. Others suggested leaving keys at work over the weekend or for locked guys to mail keys to themselves.

Another suggested buying a quantity of similar padlocks and mixing up the keys, selecting one at a time, over periods varying from a few hours to a few weeks. One guy suggested putting the keys in an envelope and leaving them with a friendly neighbor (as if for an emergency) without saying what they were for.

As with aspects of solo bondage, safety should never be forgotten. Having responsibility for another can make this a greater priority than only thinking about oneself, so the guidance regarding *Emergencies* may be particularly pertinent for those who lock themselves.

TEASING

Dominants who want to tease locked guys through discomfort or even pain are probably – like so much – only limited by their imaginations. In essence, teasing is getting someone sexually excited – and then denying them the 'relief' of an (ejaculatory) orgasm.

For some, it just adds to the fun. They enjoy being in chastity more because sexual excitement is encouraged and then frustrated; nothing more, nothing less. For others, the psychology is more complex. They find themselves more eager to serve, to submit and to be used sexually when they are aroused; they strive for a climax, even though it won't be their own, and put more energy into that. For such men, the pleasure is far more vicarious.

At its simplest, teasing need be no more than a quick reminder from the keyholder to the locked guy, whether they are together walking along a street or by an electronic message of some sort. The tone could be generous and romantic or less refined, such as 'My cock's free; yours isn't'. In his 2014 workshop in the US, Locked57 – who runs the lockedmen.net website – suggested that keyholders should communicate with locked guys, telling them how much (sexual) pleasure they are enjoying while the locked guy is experiences deprivation of one sort or another.

He also put forward the notion that sexual play – without removing a chastity device – can add to the teasing as can watching porn or reading erotic stories. Some doms may get locked guys to play with or serve others, perhaps with fairly strict restrictions on what they are allowed, or not allowed, to do. Encouraging self-stimulation while locked, perhaps in person, or on the phone or 'on cam' on the internet using sex toys to arouse the nipples, butt or balls may also be options.

Physical teasing can be achieved by creating sensations that (simultaneously) mix the extremes of agony and ecstasy. For example, the intensity that results whenever any astringent is applied to the sensitive skin of the genitals may be amplified for those who are locked. Such substances could be applied before a guy is locked – or judiciously afterwards. How long such intensity persists depends on several variables – the amount of the astringent applied, where it is put and the delicacy of the flesh. As no two guys are the same, what causes agony for one may only mildly affect another. The viscosity of the substance may also need to be considered as, for example, petroleum jelly containing menthol will probably take longer to be absorbed than a thinner hot chilli sauce, but the resulting sensation could then be described as 'chronic' rather than 'acute'. Such astringents are unlikely to cause lasting physical damage – but the intensity of the sensation can be psychologically quite terrifying, especially the first time. Once a guy has become accustomed to the feeling of burning, he can learn how long it lasts and discover ways of enduring – or perhaps even enjoying – the intensity. Like so much, context is all – and the experience is one which is probably best shared; one Dom may, for example, appreciate a guy writhing and groaning, perhaps even screaming, while another gains more pleasure from seeing a man trying to cope with the sensation in silence and motionless. An alternative suggested by another dom involves coating the cock in a thick lubricant and then adding salt or sand before telling the sub to masturbate while another suggested using emery paper – but with the additional advice that the resulting damage should be allowed time to heal before relocking or that the cock is monitored carefully for any infection. Again, the only limit to the ingenuity is the imagination ....

'THE TESTOSTERONE HUMP'

Ejaculation temporarily reduces the amount of testosterone in a man's system, so guys who get 'frequent release' will not experience a build-up of the hormone within their bodies. It can, and will, be replaced fairly quickly, according to each person's individual metabolism. Without release, more will be retained.

For many guys that translates into a more active libido; they become hornier, wanting more sex – a dimension of chastity that can be exploited for another's pleasure. However, the build-up of testosterone can have other psychological effects, best compared to mild 'roid rage'. After a period of time, a body that has previously been allowed frequent testosterone release will become accustomed to more, but hormones affect the brain too. So, while in the short period before a guy's body gets accustomed this adjustment, it may be that he experiences a mild form of 'roid rage' – being short-tempered, irritable, snappy, and so on. No two guys react the same way, but the effect on behavior is worth knowing about – not least because avoiding being too brusque can have unfortunate social and professional consequences.

Dealing with one's emotions while in chastity is probably more of a practicality of locked life than an aspect of the underlying psychology. Indeed, questions have been asked about how it can affect someone's emotional stability. For some, being locked can take someone further into the submissive role than they perhaps had initially intended. This may be OK for a few days, but after a few weeks, the wider implications of apparent personality changes may – as with many aspects of chastity – affect someone's working life. While someone who is in a position of workplace authority may become more deferential over time, shorter-term implications can affect one's behavior, especially in how someone relates to their co-workers. One guy, who is locked 'from time to time' has reported that while he loves the devotion, teasing and constant horniness, this can, he said, turn into a 'bad trip', where he experiences unpleasant, destructive frustration, neglect, rejection and being short-tempered. This is not, he said, 'generally who I am'.

One man, who had been locked for 14 years, confirmed that such feelings were possible, 'early in the experience' while another said he had known someone who had taken bolt cutters to a lock after just a few days. 'Anger, the first said, 'can result from frustration' and getting past that can take a while. Adjusting, he suggested, could take a while.

As with so much, when emotions are being explored, the best advice is probably to be aware of what could happen and what others have reported so that both the keyholder and someone who is locked can monitor feelings. If the intensity becomes destructive, action can be taken. One approach may be to unlock, allow some release and then relock, gradually extending the locking periods. This could be, at first, just by adding a day each time and then, when the emotions have become more manageable and the situation has improved, by a week.

TOILETS

Perhaps the greatest change that a guy experiences when being locked for the first time comes when they need to piss.

For most devices, using a urinal is no longer possible, although pissing into either very large, open 'trenches' or much smaller curved ones which offer some privacy may still be achievable. However, getting rid of the last drips may not be as easy as sitting down in a cubicle and using toilet tissue.

Logically, directing the urine flow from a distance towards a toilet bowl becomes far more difficult when you're wearing a cage device and impossible in a full belt. Some guys *can* stand and direct the flow so that it doesn't run down over the balls and into any clothing while standing to use some designs of urinal – usually huge stalls against a wall rather than ceramic receptacles. However, for most, the most convenient and less messy way is to sit.

This, for some, in itself represents a challenge to long-held and deep-seated perceptions of masculinity. Men, they feel, stand to piss; women sit. Others feel that the difference between the one who stands and the one who must sit is a manifestation of the power dynamic. Doms may like knowing that a submissive has to sit – because the process is more time-consuming and, until it becomes second nature, be a repeated reminder of the power exchange too. (Revenge, of a sort, can come when a guy who is wearing a kilt in the open air needs to piss; all he needs to do is spread his legs a little and 'let go'. Unlike anyone wearing trousers, he won't even have to bother with a fly.)

Guys who sit may have to shake themselves more to get rid of the last few drips and even use toilet tissue to remove urine from the outside of a device before doing up their trousers. A guy whose penis is shorter than a silicon device may also need to push a little toilet tissue into the end to remove any residue rather than experience potential embarrassment from wet spots on trousers a few moments later.

Drips seem inevitable with almost every device, so guys who would otherwise sleep naked often choose some sort of underwear rather than have to launder bedding more often than usual. For those who appreciate diapers, chastity devices can provide an excuse for indulging this predilection too.

Problems can come with pissing if a device is too tight, especially against the urethra behind the ballsac and along the perineum. Also, the 'angle of the dangle' may be such that, after sitting down, a guy still finds he has to stand and shake the device so that the final dribble emerges. Without care, this can be messy. Generally, guys who are locked will probably use more toilet tissue than those who are not!

Additionally, using urinals has become – as more toilets incorporate more open designs – more public than in heavy late 19th century china 'stalls; each almost encircling the users. Using urinals without devices being noticed has, consequently, grown increasingly difficult.

TRAINING AND LEARNING

Simply buying the first device you see, locking it in place and then hoping for a life of denial may seem exciting, but as this book shows, the realities of chastity are not so simple or straightforward.

Chastity seems to be not about sexual denial, per se, but about sexual (re-)direction. For guys who have been accustomed to anything sexual that has focused on ejaculatory orgasms, challenging the energy and aiming for a different target takes time to achieve. Thinking about this as a period of training or learning may be helpful.

Anecdotal experience seems to suggest that the first couple of days of locking followed by another period between a week and two weeks later (see 'The Testosterone Hump' in this section) are probably the most intense challenges for those locking for the first time.

Some keyholders or doms like to exploit the 'testosterone hump', only letting guys be locked to the point of greatest frustration before allowing release soon after that.

Some suggest being locked for the first time at the end of the working week, so allowing frustration to develop over the weekend and some familiarity with the device to develop before work again. Others advocate locking when life is very busy, so wearers can get through the first few days with plenty of distractions and avoid thinking about the chastity too much.

Keyholders can provide useful psychological support during these first days – encouraging rather than teasing a locked guy, taking an interest in his state of mind, his physical comfort and helping with the change of focus. Balancing anal stimulation with locking could be tried too. Some guys may find this too sexually exciting in the early days while others report that using a butt plug, for example, helps them think more about the sexual potential of that part of their anatomy rather than the genitals.

Others' writings have suggested that it is not just 'ownership' of the sexual release that is being transferred from the locked guy to the keyholder, but possession of the entire genitalia.

In one piece of writing that has been so widely circulated between various websites that the identity of the original author is difficult to trace, a training regimen is described which introduces increasingly strict restrictions on sexual release. It gives the impression of being written as a way in which chastity can be used as preparation for a power relationship rather than for introducing orgasm and sexual restriction in an existing bond.

The author advocates stopping masturbating at the very moment at which the instructions are first read. He combines becoming accustomed to chastity with concentrating on developing submissive tendencies. His approach includes linguistic prompts – such as removing the personal pronoun from any association with the genitals and using more formal terminology such as 'the penis' rather than 'my cock' as they belong to the (eventual) dominant rather than 'you'. They should, he implies, be treated with the respect and care you would afford another person's property.

He advocates wearing jockstraps – in a color that best matches the wearer's skin tone as dark against white 'contains too much power' and that contrast reflects authority. 'Part of the idea of chastity is humility,' he says, and you can't be humble with power.' After that, jockstraps are worn all day every day as such submissives never need access to the genitalia. He even advocates bathing or showering in a jock and only removing wet ones to dry and then dress again, covering the genitals with a towel while this is done so that they are out of sight.

Simple rules follow – not touching the penis, certainly not while it is erect, no passive penetrative sex and no penile stimulation. He suggests that putting a thong, chain or collar around the wrist or neck will remind a submissive of his duty to himself and a future dominant.

Pissing must take place sitting down – or even through the jock in the shower, he says. Any sexual urge should be redirected to a more 'useful' purpose, such as weight training, while visualizing the 'jing' (the Chinese philosophical concept of reverence or righteousness) coming from the testes to the entire body, enhancing the benefits of the exercise.

Every violation should initially increase the period of chastity by a day, the author suggests, while those who are more advanced should add three days each time they experience an erection. Written or edited as instructions to a specific submissive, a dominant has added a request for additional information to be provided daily – include details of any erections, an assessment of horniness (ranked from zero to 10) and taking his temperature each morning and evening using a rectal thermometer.

Another published writer – 'Squaddie John' – has written that discipline for a male submissive includes cock control as the penis is 'unpredictable when untrained'. Masturbation, he says, leads to 'unpredictable motivation, moods swings and poor performance'. His ideal is a submissive whose balls are full, whose cock 'is half hand when resting, ready to spring to attention when required and then shoot to order'.

He has also described techniques for cock control but warns that 'manipulating sexual responses can be cruel and cause dependency or behavioral changes that are difficult to reverse'. In terms of physical control, he suggests that the less one achieves orgasm, the less it is desired and it becomes more difficult to achieve. Masturbation is acceptable – but within the control of the dominant, not the submissive.

UNLOCKING

So, what does or can happen when a guy is released and allowed to become fully erect and potential ejaculate for the first time after being locked for a few weeks? Some men enjoy their freedom without reporting any adverse effects – but this should not be taken for granted.

One guy reported online that he found that the 'first passage of semen' after a period of abstinence 'could be painful', perhaps, he mused because of the 40-day locking period but also the thickness and bulk of the load that had accumulated.

The responses were varied. One guy suggested drinking lots of water to dilute the seminal fluid with the combination of as much teasing as possible before eventual release. Another advised having a bath while a third thought that at ruined orgasm every 20 days or so might help. A fourth said that it may take a few hours to attain a full and hard erection or that ejaculation may occur exceedingly quickly, even before the locked guy realized it was happening. (Others have reported that 'strong' erections do return after long periods of locking – but that this can take several days and repeated masturbation.)

A further contributor suggested that the fastest way to (re-hydrate) is to use a fresh water enema. This should, he said, be held for no more than 20 minutes and purified, rather than tap or distilled, water should be used. He also suggested that using a sound to stretch the urethra. That may either slightly weaken the internal membranes or increase the flexibility should the seminal fluid still be thick.

(Douching may remove some mucus from internal membranes but is a practical alternative to holding an enema as a way of hydrating the body. Care should always be taken when inserting tap water into the rectum or the genitals, especially in locations where water quality standards cannot be taken for granted. Microscopic impurities that may be quickly destroyed by gastric juices and the powerful acids of the digestive system may be absorbed anally – causing potential discomfort or even sickness.)

Sitting in water in the bath may have some effect – but the quantity of blood circulating around that part of the body means that internal temperatures may be hotter than the water. Warming the water used in an enema make help thin seminal fluid lurking in the prostate.

Others also reported experiencing pain during the first ejaculation after a period of abstinence; one guy said that, when he was in his 'horny teen years' this could happen within 48 hours while another had felt that his first orgasm after 44 days was painful. The dominant had, generously, allowed a second, more pleasurable, release an hour later.

URETHRAL PROBES/PLUGS

These additions to chastity devices need to be used with care. Introducing anything into the penis does have potential risks – especially as the thin membrane of the urethra can relatively easily be damaged during movement. Clearly, the possibility of this is directly related to the workmanship of the device – so those with rougher edges or made of less pure materials are best avoided.

Cleanliness is important too as it may be possible – depending on what has been happening – for seminal fluid to accumulate between the metal tube and the urethra that is not washed away during urination. Internal bruising or other damage may heal quickly and almost unnoticed once a plug is removed, but infections can occur.

Medicine has a generic term – urinary tract infection (UTI) – but does not appear to differentiate between those which may be sexually transmitted or the result of physical damage. Should blood ever appear in urine while a probe or plug is in place, it should be removed immediately. If, after drinking an ample quantity of water, blood is evident again, the best advice is probably to seek medical attention. In the UK, major hospitals have departments of Genito-Urinary (GU) Medicine – which primarily deal with sexually transmitted infections (STIs). The staff are accustomed to confidentiality and discretion and have probably 'seen it all before', so while these may not be open or available 24-hours a day like an emergency room, they could be preferable alternative to these or primary care physicians or general practitioners (GPs).

Being sensible applies to all urethral play – whether it is the use of probes that are not attached to chastity devices, to sounds or to catheters. Before anything is inserted, it should be as clean as possible, if not sterile – and introduced using copies quantities of sterile lubricant. Once a tube of lube is open it will no longer be sterile. Boxes of sachets of sterile lube are widely available in pharmacies or online.

While again, little if any formal medical guidance is available, common sense would suggest that, depending on how active someone is being, probes and urethral plugs are only left in place for hours rather than days. The sensation, especially of the prostate by a long probe, may be wonderful – but the potential for internal damage should not be underestimated.

WEIGHT

Losing or gaining weight can be impractical for those being locked into 'full belts'. While many of the designs now have ways of accommodating some changes, these are not great. Those whose weight fluctuates may consider cage designs as being more practical.

Look at manufacturers' websites and the men modelling devices, especially, full belts can be broad of shoulder and narrow of waist. Most guys are not like that. Ergonomic waistband designs, which are intended to 'sit' on the hips, have been welcomed in online reports from bigger men. One man commented that he was overweight, about 22 stone (nearly 310 pounds or 140 kilos) and 5ft 9ins (173 cms) tall before saying that he had configured his belt so that is sat low on his hips and under his belt. That was, he said, 'comfortable and practical'.

Another 'very overweight' guy confessed that being heavy interfered with security. 'The extra padding around the pelvis,' he said, ' means you have less of your penis sticking out and into a tube, so it is easier to pull out.'

Some have advised that making sure that you can stay at a reasonably constant weight for a year is sensible before paying for an expensive, custom-made full belt. This is because, in many climates, our eating patterns – and consequent body weight and fat ratios – vary with the seasons and the amount of exercise that we do.

WORSHIP

Although the dynamics of a relationship in which worship is a part may appear, to the unknowing, as very unbalanced and even the personification or manifestation of unrequited love, this is frequently far from the truth. Offering a key to someone may comprise part of a worship relationship – with benefits for both.

Developing your sexual technique for another person's pleasure is paramount. Learning and remembering to use fingers and toes, all your mouth – including the tongue and lips – to stimulate another person's body is vital. Learn about anatomy and where nerve endings are most concentrated – but don't forget that the delight of gentleness to one is the agony of tickling for another. Being locked, so that the temptation to stimulate oneself is removed, can enhance worship – by ensuring that there is no competition for the sexual focus, combined with the built-up horniness achieved after a period of restriction. Being locked also manifests the dynamic – showing that the submissive's release is secondary to that of the person being worshipped.

In these circumstances, the keyholder is monarch and deity, to be afforded the same respect, adoration and obedience as the most oppressed subject or devoted acolyte. After all, the words discipline and disciple are really the same.

Afterthought
THE QUESTIONS CONTINUE

Chastity seems – after several tens of thousands of words – to be as much about questions as answers.

The scope for serious, proper, peer-reviewed research remains – but with questions about how would 'come out' as potential peers to review such work and the personal credence they could bring to such assessments.

What questions should those be? Some were missing from the survey carried out on the Lockedmen website in 2014.

Personally, after writing all this, I would be fascinated to know:

- Is cash a significant factor in influencing which device you choose?
- Roughly how much would you consider spending on a device?
- Do you think being in chastity influences your behavior? If so how?
- Are you a 'grower' or a 'show-er'?
- Do you feel that your penis size is affected by being locked? If so how?
- Can you get erect while locked?
- Are you circumcised?
- Do you have any penis piercings? If yes, which?
- Do you have any other genital modifications?
- Do you have to unlock for hygiene reasons?
- How do you keep clean while you are locked?
- How large are you flaccid? Erect?
- Did the size of your penis influence your choice of device?

- Can you achieve 'orgasm' while locked?
- Can you/have you ejaculated while being locked?
- Do you use add-ons, such as a Kali's Teeth Bracelet or 'points of intrigue', to deter erections?
- Is the aim of your chastity to:
- Prevent penetration of another?
- Prevent masturbation?
- Prevent erection?
- Prevent your own penetration?
- What do you in terms of prostate health?

Sufficient answers to these questions would at least enable the offerings and thoughts reported here to be substantiated a little more thoroughly, transferring them some of the way from being purely anecdotal to being validated by numbers.

Additionally, knowing why – for example – individuals became interested in chastity and 'got into it' would be fascinating as would finding out about what it 'does' for individuals and what they get out of it. Is chastity 'enjoyed' or experienced as part of a (power) relationship or merely as a prelude to (intense) sexual activity or other SM 'play'?

The Lockedmen research found out a little about the devices being used, but discovering more about the reasons behind each choice would be helpful too, especially to the manufacturers.

Experiences with longer periods of locking seem particularly worthwhile – as both reports of problems and accounts of joys are appreciated by others.

Each and every one of us has our own 'chastity story'; telling them would allow us to find out how much we have in common and where we disagree. The research done for this book goes some way to offer some evidence, but one important axiom remains: the more we learn then the more we can enjoy.

ABOUT THE AUTHOR

Christopher Charlton is nearly 60 and has been interested in power relationships and SM for more than 40 years. He is a professional writer and journalist, covering health, including HIV, and the media. He takes his play and relationships seriously, being a long-standing member of a leading SM club in the US. He read psychology at university in England.

Chris's interests include many aspects of physical SM, the exploration of the body and its responses. He is also intrigued by the ways in which finding and being open about the power dynamics between people can keep the most intimate relationships alive and exciting.

His novella trilogy – *Revelation, Renaissance and Retirement; a slave's voyage of Self-Discovery* – was published by EmOhErotica in 2015. They are available in Kindle format from Amazon. Chris says he takes inspiration from leading writers such as John Preston, 'Fledermaus', Race Bannon, Joseph Bean and Guy Baldwin, and looks for the beautiful, the positive and the inspirational in the honesty that allows people to appreciate the power dynamics of dominance and willing submission.

You can contact him by e-mail: chrschrltn@gmail.com

DISCLAIMER

The information presented in this book is for personal interest only. Performing any of the activities or behaviors mentioned here is at the reader's own risk. The author and publisher cannot accept any responsibility for activities and behaviors described here. Care is advised at all times as is seeking qualified medical guidance wherever and whenever appropriate. Details of the US-based Kink Aware Professionals network can be found online.